THE NEW STATE OF WAR AND PEACE

THE NEW STATE OF WAR AND PEACE

AN INTERNATIONAL ATLAS

A Full Color Survey of Arsenals, Armies and Alliances
Throughout the World

Michael Kidron and Dan Smith

A Pluto Project

A TOUCHSTONE BOOK
Published by Simon & Schuster Inc.
New York

Simon and Schuster/Touchstone Books,
Published by Simon & Schuster Inc.
Simon & Schuster Building
Rockefeller Center
1230 Avenue of the Americas
New York, New York 10020

SIMON AND SCHUSTER, TOUCHSTONE and colophons
are registered trademarks of Simon & Schuster Inc.

Published in Great Britain
by Grafton Books, a division of HarperCollins

Artwork for maps by Swanston Graphics Limited, Derby, England

Artwork and typesetting by James Mills-Hicks, Isabelle Verpeaux, Andrea
Fairbrass, Jacqueline Land, Jeanne Radford, Virginia McFadyen,
Pamela Hopkinson, Adrian van Weerdenburg and Malcolm Swanston

Design by Grundy & Northedge, London

Coordinated by Anne Benewick

Produced by Mandarin Offset
Printed and bound in Hong Kong

10   9   8   7   6   5   4   3   2   1
10   9   8   7   6   5   4   3   2   1   Pbk.

Library of Congress Cataloging in Publication Data

Kidron, Michael
    The new state of war and peace: an international atlas:
    a full color survey of arsenals, armies and alliances
    throughout the world / Michael Kidron and Dan Smith
    p. cm.

    Artwork for maps by Swanston Graphics Limited, Derby, England
    –Verso t.p.
    "A Pluto Project."
    "A Touchstone book."

    ISBN 0-671-70521-0: $27.95.—ISBN 0-671-70103-7 (pbk.): $14.95

    1. War—Maps.   2. Military history, Modern—20th century—Maps.
    3. World politics—1945.   4. Arms race.   I. Smith, Dan.
    II. Swanston Graphics Limited.   III. Title

G1048.R1K47   1991   ‹G&M›
355′.009′048022—dc20

90-22780
CIP
MAP

CONTENTS

WAR FAIR

COSTS

INTRODUCTION

Hope can flourish in the most unpropitious conditions and there are times and places when anything not only seems but is possible. Such a time and such a place was eastern Europe in 1989. The pace of history quickened, people rose, walls fell, a corrupt and repressive system collapsed. In a few intense months an end came to a global political order based on Cold War confrontation which had seemed immoveable and irreducible.

It appeared then that a more benign order could emerge. The end of the 1980s had brought a close to some wars, a slackening of others. Wars of intervention and conflict between states declined in number. The civil wars which continued were often just as brutal — sometimes worse — but at least they carried less threat to life outside the immediate war zone.

On the other side of hope, disappointment may lie. In 1990 the pace of history barely slowed but the pace of peace-making did. In Africa, Latin America and Asia — almost everywhere except Europe and North America, in fact — the dogs of war continued to snarl and savage. In the middle of 1990 came the Iraqi invasion and annexation of Kuwait, followed by a swift multinational military response. It began to seem that the new order might prove a great deal less benign than had been hoped.

The old order, which now lies buried beneath the Berlin Wall that was its richest and most ambiguous symbol — buried by the people, not the strategists or the politicians — derived from a seemingly fundamental and irreducible conflict between the two power blocs led by the USA and the USSR. Only a few states managed to stand aside from this bi-polar world order across more than four decades. Politically, its logic was to be all-consuming, tending to absorb all other antagonisms within it; militarily, had Cold War become hot, it would have *been* all-consuming — the nuclear arms race had produced the instruments of total destruction.

We could not, as we finished preparing this atlas, know how the new order would turn out. If it is shaped by the 1990 crisis in the Gulf, it may, like the old, be well-armed and prone to war or, at least, military risk-taking. But there would be two differences. New enemies would draw different lines of conflict and confrontation. And, unlike the Cold War, the new order will not — at least for a time, if ever — threaten total annihilation in total war. Whether there would be other ways in which the new order might be genuinely more peaceful than the old was, at the time of writing, unclear.

The events that unfolded during the time in which we conceived, 7 researched and prepared this atlas — we began planning in September 1988 and finished doing in September 1990 — have repeatedly brought to mind the Chinese ideogram for 'crisis'. It is a combination of two other characters: that for 'danger' and that for 'opportunity'. Scanning the world that we attempted to depict, even as it changed and in its changing lights, at different moments and in different places, we saw here more danger, there more opportunity, now a fine balance between them, next a collapse into disaster.

Between the old protagonists of the Cold War, the dominant theme is opportunity and the primary question is how fully and far-sightedly it will be exploited. But elsewhere — most notably in the Middle East, but also in parts of Asia, Africa and Latin America — danger has been dominant. And perhaps in Cambodia, South Africa and the USSR, the balance has been at its finest; in each, with great gains possible on one side, and great disasters possible on the other, the outcome remained unclear. Attempting to catch, as it does, both the openings and the pitfalls for peace, this atlas depicts a world on the cusp of change, poised between an old, known order and a new one as yet unformed, of which we can glimpse different possible silhouettes, whose details are far from clear.

We have also been struck by another piece of Chinese wisdom, an ancient curse, 'May you live in interesting times'. Statistics and much other data are never available immediately. Standard reference books, annually published, display the previous year's statistics where they are known, which is by no means always. As we retail those figures through a visual and thus, we hope, more accessible presentation, we confront our readers with data which are perhaps two years old when we appear. Such time-lags are unimportant when world politics are relatively stable. But when we live in interesting times, they become more weighty.

While we have been working on this atlas, two pairs of states — the two Germanies and the two Yemens — have united, while the full territorial extent and current borders of the USSR, Yugoslavia and Canada have come into question. At the same time, one of the world's two major military alliances, the Warsaw Pact, went into a rapid, terminal decline. Arms reduction talks and ceasefire negotiations with real chances of success — but also real risks of failure — offered hope for the world and the threat of outdated data for us. For just as the suddenly quickening pace of history has made all interpretation of it necessarily provisional, so it makes all factual depiction of it necessarily more tentative.

For the sake of consistent presentation, we have occasionally provided information on states which no longer exist (showing, for example, what they spent on armed forces in 1989), and on an alliance which had no meaning. We have taken internationally recognized states with their names and borders as of mid-1989, except Germany where we have recognized unification in October 1990 wherever possible. Where unfolding changes have affected the subject matter of the maps, we have attempted to deal with them in the notes at the end of the atlas. They are designed to be read with the maps and may reveal to the reader, either directly or implicitly, some of the intellectual and informational exploration and survey work we undertook in order to produce the maps.

Many people have helped in the making of this book. We wish to thank them. Some are acknowledged on page 10 for their contribution to our research and our understanding. There are others who helped in that way but would feel uncomfortable with a public acknowledgement; they know who they are, and know they have our unreserved thanks. We also wish to thank people who are so at the heart of the project that gratitude is virtually superfluous. The team at Swanston Graphics, under the leadership of Malcolm Swanston, provided inspired design and cartography. As project co-ordinator, Anne Benewick was creative, efficient and surprisingly cheerful. Finally, we wish to thank each other for providing company, support and illumination in charting these complicated waters.

Michael Kidron
Dan Smith

London & Brighton
September 1990

ACKNOWLEDGEMENTS

We would not have been able to complete — nor would we have even dared to begin — the research for many of the maps in this atlas without the help of many people. Some are old friends and colleagues of many years, some we met only when we asked for their help — and some of them we know only by their telephone voice. Some helped guide us through minefields of unclear data and blurred definitions, others provided us with specific facts, or alerted us to data, or directed us towards sources of which we had previously been unaware. Some spent hours advising us and clarifying problems, or equally long in digging out recondite information from the depths of their research files and libraries. Others answered a phone call, gave us a reference, suggested the name of somebody else who could help, and variously gave or lent us press clippings, journals, books, computer print-outs and highly specialized publications of which only a few dozen copies exist. Some fixed our computer programmes (or told us how not to panic). Whatever they did, we thank them all, unreservedly, and wish — with some exceptions, in order to avoid embarrassing them — to acknowledge their generosity:—

Mary Acland-Hood; Mariano Aquirre, Centro de Investigacion para la Paz, Madrid; Hayward R Alker, jr, Massachusetts Institute of Technology, Cambridge, Ma.; Peter Andreas, Institute for Policy Studies, Washington, DC (IPS); Ian Anthony, Stockholm International Peace Research Institute (SIPRI); Patricia Ardila, The Panos Institute, Washington, DC; Derek Ballington, Janes Publishing Co; Anthony Barnett, *New Statesman and Society*, London; Billie Bielckus, SIPRI; Hans Binnendijk, International Institute for Strategic Studies, London (IISS); Frank Blackaby; Fiona Bristow, Population Concern, London; Yogesh Chandrani; Philip Chrimes, Royal Institute of International Affairs, London; Michael Crawley, Imperial College, London; Christopher Davis, Centre of Russian & East European Studies, Birmingham; Pria Dershingkar, Sussex University; Saadet Deger, SIPRI; Neven Dragojlovic, American School, Tangier; Nick Dunlop; Felicity Ehrlich, Refugee Studies Programme, Oxford (RSP); Denis Galagher, Refugee Policy Group, Washington, DC; Susan George, Transnational Institute, Amsterdam (TNI)) Jo Graham, Africa Watch, London; Richard Guthrie, Sussex University; Fred Halliday, London School of Economics (LSE); Robert Harkavy, Pennsylvania State University; Barbara Harrell-Bond, RSP; Warwick Harris, British Refugee Council, London; Mike Hassel, Imperial College, London; Bill Hetherington, Peace Pledge Union, London; Keith Hindell, United Nations Information Centre, London (UNIC); Jochen Hippler, TNI, Amsterdam and Institute for International Relations, Wuppertal; Hugh Hudson, United Nations High Commission for Refugees (UNHCR), London; Kay Johnson, Hampshire College, Amherst, Ma.; Don Kerr, IISS; Saul Landaum IPS; Chris Langford, LSE; Michael Leifer, LSE; Emmanuel Mack, RSP; Roger Matthews, *Financial Times*; Juan Mendes, Americas Watch, Washington, DC; Martin McCusker; Ed Mickolus, Vinyard Software Inc, Falls Church, Va.; Carol Moor, US Committee on Refugees, Washington, DC; Nicholas Morris, UNHCR, Geneva; Peter Moszynski, Africa Confidential, London; Geoff Murell, Research Department, Foreign & Commonwealth Office, London; Roger Naumann, Oxfam; Office of Population Censuses and Surveys, London; Sasha Pears, Amnesty International (AI); Julian Perry Robinson, Sussex

University; Mario Pianta; Dan Plesch, British-American Security Information Council, London/Washington; Joel Rocamora, TNI; Roc Sandford; Ronald Segal; Robert Shuey, Congressional Research Service, Washington, DC; Nicholas Sims, LSE; Jeremy Smith, Royal Geographical Society Map Room, London; Ron Smith, Birkbeck College, London; David Snoxell, British Information Service, New York; Rob Somerville; Kaye Stearman, Minority Rights Group, London; Marion Storkey, Population Concern, London; Doron Swade; Ann Thirkell-Smith, RSP; Hans Thoden, UNHCR, Geneva; the Treaty Section of the Foreign and Commonwealth Office, London; Debby Trevor, AI; Francis Tusa; Stanley Uys; Achin Vinaik, *Times of India*, Bombay; Alex de Waal, Africa Watch, London; Alex Walden, UNHCR, London; Martin Walton, UNIC; Julian de Wette, UNIC; Jill Wilcox, UNICEF, London; Paul Wilkinson, St Andrew's University, Scotland; Ken Wilson, RSP; Lewis Wolpert; Herbert Wulf, SIPRI.

We benefited also from the skilled assistance of library staff, whom we also wish to thank for their labours. They are:—

Lynn Baker & Sarah Booker, Foreign Office Library; Alison Duffield, Imperial War Museum Library; Susan Baker, Hilary Oakley & Carolyn Wells, International Institute for Strategic Studies Library, London; Edwin Trout & David Wileman, Royal Geographical Society Library, London; Susan Boyd, Jenny Foreman, Nicole Gallimore, Maggie Julien, John Pell, Liz Parcell, Royal Institute of International Affairs Library; John Montgomery, Royal United Services Institute Library, London; Staff of the British Library, Business Information Service; Staff of the Royal Borough of Kensington and Chelsea Public Library; Staff of the University of Sussex Library; Staff of the Hampshire College and Amherst College Libraries, Amherst, Ma.

A DECADE OF WARS

In this atlas we have regarded an open armed conflict as war if:
- regular armed forces are engaged on at least one side;
- the fighters and fighting are organized centrally to some extent;
- there is some continuity between clashes.

The following table shows all states involved in war at any stage between January 1980 and September 1990. It does not distinguish between different civil wars where several are going on simultaneously: as in China, India, Indonesia, Myanmar (Burma), the Philippines and South Africa.

Many wars appear twice in the table; for example, the war in Afghanistan appears as a civil war and also as a war of intervention by the USSR; the war in Lebanon is a civil war and also, for four other states, a war of intervention.

The distinction between interstate and interventionary war is often so blurred that we have shown them as one category.

The difficulties of defining precisely when wars start and end, and the issues involved in defining war, are discussed in the note to Map 4: *The Dogs of War*.

Sources:

Keesing's Register of World Events, Harlow: Longman, annual; *The Europa World Yearbook 1989*, London: Europa Publications, 1989; Brogan, P., *World Conflicts*, London: Bloomsbury, 1989; Kohn, G.C., *Dictionary of Wars*, New York: Doubleday, 1987; Degenhardt H.W., *Revolutionary and Dissident Movements, An International Guide*, Harlow: Longman, 1988; Starr R.F. ed., *Yearbook on International Communist Affairs*, Stanford: Hoover Institution, 1987; Hobday C., *Communist and Marxist Parties of the World*, Harlow: Longman, 1986; Humana, C., *World Human Rights Guide*, 2nd edn., London: Pan, 1987; *Strategy Survey*, successive years, London: International Institute for Strategic Studies; *World Armaments & Disarmament: SIPRI Yearbook*, 1989, 1990 eds., Oxford: Oxford University Press, 1989, 1990; Sivard, R.L., *World Military & Social Expenditures 1989*, Washington, DC: World Priorities Inc, 1989; Wallensteen, P., ed., *States in Armed Conflict 1988*, Uppsala: Uppsala University, July 1989; press reports.

		War began	War ended
Afghanistan	intervention by USSR	1978	1989
Angola	intervention by Cuba & South Africa	1975	war continuing 1990
Argentina		1976	1982
Argentina	against United Kingdom	1982	1982
Bangladesh		1975	war continuing 1990
Bolivia		1985	war continuing 1990
Burkina Faso	against Mali	1986	1986
Burundi		1988	1988
Cambodia	intervention by Vietnam	1970	war continuing 1990
Chad		1965	war continuing 1990
Chad	against Libya	1981	1981
Chad	against Libya	1983	1983
Chad	against Libya	1986	1988
China		1983	1984
China	against Vietnam	1987	1987
China		1987	war continuing 1990
Colombia		1986	war continuing 1990
Cuba	against Unita rebels & South Africa in Angola	1975	1988
Ecuador	against Peru	1981	1983
El Salvador		1979	war continuing 1990
Ethiopia		1962	war continuing 1990
Ethiopia	against Somalia	1977	1988
France		1977	war continuing 1990
France	in Lebanon	1982	1984
France	against Libya	1983	1983
France	against Libya	1986	1987
France	in New Caledonia	1988	1988
Gambia		1981	1981
Ghana		1981	1981
Grenada	intervention by USA	1983	1983
Guatemala		1968	war continuing 1990
Honduras		1981	1981
Honduras	against Nicaragua	1983	1983
Honduras	against Nicaragua	1986	1986
Honduras	against Nicaragua	1988	1988
India		1947	war continuing 1990
India	against Tamil Tigers in Sri Lanka	1987	1990
Indonesia		1975	war continuing 1990

interstate war including intervention | civil war | civil war with intervention

13

		War began	War ended
Iran		1978	war continuing 1990
Iran	against Iraq	1980	1988
Iraq		1974	1989
Iraq	against Iran	1980	1988
Iraq	against Kuwait	1990	war continuing 1990
Israel		1948	war continuing 1990
Israel	in Lebanon	1980	1980
Israel	in Lebanon	1982	1982
Korea, South		1980	1980
Kuwait	against Iraq	1990	war continuing 1990
Laos	against Thailand	1975	1988
Laos	intervention by Vietnam	1977	1988
Lebanon	intervention by Syria (1976–), Israel (1980 & 1982), France & USA (1982-84)	1975	war continuing 1990
Liberia		1985	1985
Liberia		1989	war continuing 1990
Libya	against Tunisia	1980	1980
Libya	against Chad	1981	1981
Libya	against Chad & France	1983	1983
Libya	against Chad & France (1986-87)	1986	1988
Malaysia		1948	1989
Mali	against Burkina Faso	1986	1986
Morocco	against Western Sahara	1976	war continuing 1990
Mozambique	intervention by Zimbabwe	1976	war continuing 1990
Mozambique	against Rhodesia	1976	1980
Mozambique	against South Africa	1981	1982
Myanmar (Burma)		1948	war continuing 1990
Namibia	against South Africa	1965	1988
New Caledonia	intervention by France	1988	1988
Nicaragua		1970	1990
Nicaragua	against Honduras	1983	1983
Nicaragua	against Honduras	1986	1986
Nicaragua	against Honduras	1988	1988
Nigeria		1980	1981
Nigeria		1984	1984
Pakistan		1947	war continuing 1990
Panama	against USA	1989	1989
Papua New Guinea		1989	war continuing 1990
Peru		1980	war continuing 1990
Peru	against Ecuador	1981	1983

interstate war including intervention	civil war	civil war with intervention	anti-colonial war

		War began	War ended
Philippines		1969	war continuing 1990
Romania		1989	1989
Saudi Arabia		1979	1980
Somalia		1977	war continuing 1990
Somalia	against Ethiopia	1977	1988
South Africa		1964	war continuing 1990
South Africa	against Namibia	1965	1988
South Africa	against Angola & Cuba (to 1988)	1975	1989
South Africa	against Mozambique	1981	1982
Spain		1973	war continuing 1990
Sri Lanka	intervention by India	1977	war continuing 1990
Sudan		1955	war continuing 1990
Suriname		1986	war continuing 1990
Syria	in Lebanon	1976	war continuing 1990
Syria		1982	1982
Thailand	against Laos	1975	1988
Thailand		1945	1989
Tunisia	against Libya	1980	1980
Turkey		1977	war continuing 1990
Uganda		1971	war continuing 1990
United Kingdom		1969	war continuing 1990
United Kingdom	against Argentina	1982	1982
USA	in Lebanon	1982	1984
USA	against Grenada	1983	1983
USA	against drug barons in Bolivia	1986	1986
USA	against Panama	1989	1989
USSR	against Mujahedin in Afghanistan	1979	1989
USSR		1988	war continuing 1990
Vanuatu		1980	1980
Vietnam	in Cambodia	1977	1989
Vietnam	against China	1987	1987
Western Sahara	against Morocco	1976	war continuing 1990
Yemen, South		1986	1986
Yugoslavia		1981	war continuing 1990
Zimbabwe (as Rhodesia)		1972	1980
Zimbabwe (as Rhodesia)	against Mozambique	1976	1980
Zimbabwe		1982	1983
Zimbabwe	against MNR rebels in Mozambique	1984	war continuing 1990

interstate war including intervention   civil war   civil war with intervention   colonial war

Copyright © Swanston Publishing Limited

ICELAND

FINLAND

NORWAY
SWEDEN

DENMARK

IRELAND

UNITED
KINGDOM

USA

USA
NETH

BEL

LUX

USA

GERMANY

USSR
POLAND

USSR
CZECHOSLOVAKIA

U S

US

USSR
HUNG

FRANCE

SWITZ

AUSTRIA

ROM

ITALY

YUGOSLAVIA

BU

USA

PORTUGAL

USA
SPAIN

ALBANIA

GRE
USA

GIBRALTAR (Br)

C A N A D A

UNITED STATES
OF AMERICA

BERMUDA

ATLANTIC
OCEAN

TUNISIA

MOROCCO

ALGERIA

LIB

MEXICO

BAHAMAS

WESTERN SAHARA

CUBA

HAITI
DOMINICAN REPUBLIC
PUERTO RICO (US)

MAURITANIA

MALI

NIGER

BELIZE
GUATEMALA
EL SALVADOR
HONDURAS

NICARAGUA

JAMAICA

GUADELOUPE (Fr)

DOMINICA

MARTINIQUE (Fr)

BARBADOS

CAPE VERDE

SENEGAL
GAMBIA

GUINEA-BISSAU

GUINEA

BURKINA

IVORY
COAST

GHANA

C

BENIN

NIGERIA

TOGO

COSTA RICA

PANAMA

TRINIDAD & TOBAGO

VENEZUELA

GUYANA

SURINAME

FRENCH GUIANA (Fr)

SIERRA-LEONE
LIBERIA

CAMEROON

COLOMBIA

EQUATORIAL GUINEA

SAO TOME & PRINCIPE

GABON

ECUADOR

CONGO

PERU

B R A Z I L

ANG

BOLIVIA

PACIFIC
OCEAN

PARAGUAY

NAMI

CHILE

THE DOVE OF PEACE

THE OUTBREAK OF PEACE
1988-90

states undertaking or
announcing cuts in armed
forces *mid-1990*

other states

URUGUAY

ARGENTINA

ceasefire achieved *1988-90*

ceasefire talks *1988-90*

war continues, but
disengagement by major
named combatant *1988-90*

FALKLAND ISLANDS (Br)

withdrawal from foreign
bases under way,
impending or under
negotiation, by named state
mid- 1990

Sources in notes

The world is still burdened with war and conflict, but in the late 1980s the dove of peace was sighted.

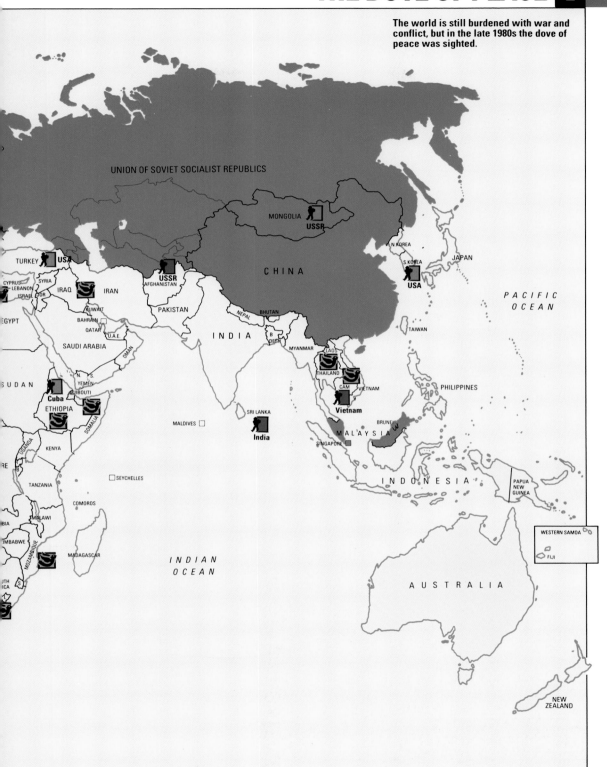

UNION OF SOVIET SOCIALIST REPUBLICS

MONGOLIA

USSR

CHINA

N KOREA

S KOREA

USA

JAPAN

TURKEY USA

USSR
AFGHANISTAN

CYPRUS
SYRIA
LEBANON
ISRAEL JOR
IRAQ

IRAN

EGYPT

KUWAIT

BAHRAIN

QATAR

U.A.E

PAKISTAN

NEPAL BHUTAN

INDIA

B
DESH

MYANMAR

LAOS

THAILAND

CAM

VIETNAM

Vietnam

PHILIPPINES

TAIWAN

PACIFIC
OCEAN

SAUDI ARABIA

OMAN

SUDAN

N. S.
YEMEN

DJIBOUTI

Cuba

ETHIOPIA

SOMALIA

UGANDA

KENYA

SRI LANKA

MALDIVES

India

MALAYSIA

SINGAPORE

BRUNEI

INDONESIA

TANZANIA

COMOROS

SEYCHELLES

PAPUA
NEW
GUINEA

MALAWI

ZIMBABWE

MOZAMBIQUE

MADAGASCAR

INDIAN
OCEAN

WESTERN SAMOA

FIJI

AUSTRALIA

UTH
ICA

NEW
ZEALAND

Copyright © Swanston Publishing Limited

ICELAND

NORWAY
SWEDEN
FINLAND

DENMARK

IRELAND
UNITED KINGDOM

NETH
BEL
LUX
GERMANY
POLAND
U S S R

Strategic arms reduction talks: USA/USSR

West Germany only

CZECHOSLOVAKIA
Vienna
AUSTRIA
HUNGARY
ROMA

FRANCE
SWITZ
LIE

Geneva conference on disarmament: 40 participants
Geneva

PORTUGAL
SPAIN

ITALY
YUGOSLAVIA
BUL

ALBANIA
GREEC

GIBRALTAR (Br)

Vienna conference on forces in Europe: NATO/Warsaw Pact state

CANADA

UNITED STATES OF AMERICA

BERMUDA

MEXICO

BAHAMAS

ATLANTIC OCEAN

CUBA
HAITI
DOMINICAN REPUBLIC
PUERTO RICO (US)
ST.KITTS-NEVIS
ANGUILLA

JAMAICA
GUADELOUPE (Fr)
ANTIGUA & BARBUDA
DOMINICA

BELIZE
GUATEMALA
HONDURAS
EL SALVADOR
COSTA RICA
NICARAGUA
ST.LUCIA
MARTINIQUE (Fr)
ST.VINCENT & THE GRENADINES
GRENADA
BARBADOS
TRINIDAD & TOBAGO

PANAMA
VENEZUELA
SURINAME
GUYANA
FRENCH GUIANA (Fr)

COLOMBIA

ECUADOR

CAPE VERDE

MOROCCO
TUNISIA
ALGERIA
LIBY

WESTERN SAHARA

MAURITANIA
MALI
NIGER
CH

SENEGAL
GAMBIA
GUINEA-BISSAU
GUINEA
BURKINA
NIGERIA

SIERRA LEONE
LIBERIA
IVORY COAST
GHANA
TOGO
BENIN
CA

EQUATORIAL GUINEA
CAMEROON
SAO TOME & PRINCIPE
GABON
CONGO

BRAZIL

PERU

BOLIVIA

PARAGUAY

CHILE

URUGUAY

ARGENTINA

FALKLAND ISLANDS (Br)

ANG

NAMIB

Inset map (Treaty Tlatelolco):

USA
GUATEMALA
BAHAMAS
HAITI
DOM REP
CUBA
BELIZE
HONDURAS
NICARAGUA
JAMAICA
ST.KITTS-NEVIS
ANTIGUA
DOMINICA
ST.LUCIA
BARBADOS
ST.VINCENT
GRENADA
TRINIDAD & TOBAGO
COSTA RICA
PANAMA
EL SALVADOR
VENEZUELA
GUYANA
SURINAME
COLOMBIA
FRENCH GUIANA (Fr)
ECUADOR
PERU
BRAZIL
BOLIVIA
PARAGUAY
CHILE
URUGUAY
ARGENTINA
FALKLAND ISLANDS (Br)

TREATY TLATELOLCO NUCLEAR-FREE ZONE
February 1990

▢ parties to Treaty Tlatelolco

▢ parties for whom treaty not yet in force

▢ non-parties

TALKS AND TREATIES

DIPLOMATIC RELATIONS
percentage change in the numbers of fully active, national missions accredited by sovereign states *1973-1989*

- 200% increase
- 100%
- 50%
- 25%
- 0
- decrease
- data not available

ARMS CONTROL TREATIES
Number of major arms control treaties (total=8) to which each state is party, *1 January 1990*

- 8
- 3–5
- 6–7
- 1–2
- ▢ none

Sources in notes

If the world seemed to be getting safer at the end of the 1980s, some of the credit belongs to expanded diplomatic relations and three decades of arms control talks. The talking and treaty-making continues.

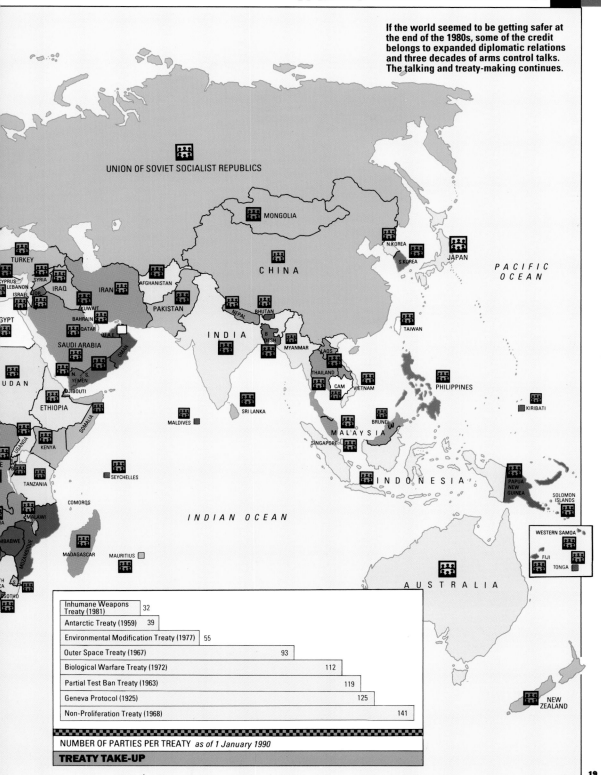

UNION OF SOVIET SOCIALIST REPUBLICS

MONGOLIA

N.KOREA

S.KOREA

JAPAN

PACIFIC OCEAN

CHINA

TURKEY

CYPRUS
LEBANON
ISRAEL
SYRIA
JOR
IRAQ
IRAN
AFGHANISTAN

GYPT

KUWAIT
BAHRAIN
QATAR
U.A.E.
SAUDI ARABIA
OMAN
N. S.
YEMEN
DJIBOUTI

PAKISTAN

NEPAL
BHUTAN

INDIA
B DESH
MYANMAR

LAOS
THAILAND
CAM
VIETNAM

TAIWAN

PHILIPPINES

KIRIBATI

UDAN

ETHIOPIA

SOMALIA

MALDIVES

SRI LANKA

BRUNEI

MALAYSIA

SINGAPORE

UGANDA
KENYA

SEYCHELLES

INDONESIA

TANZANIA

COMOROS

PAPUA
NEW
GUINEA

SOLOMON
ISLANDS

INDIAN OCEAN

MALAWI

MADAGASCAR

MAURITIUS

MBABWE
MOZAMBIQUE

TH
CA
LESOTHO

AUSTRALIA

WESTERN SAMOA

FIJI

TONGA

NEW
ZEALAND

TREATY TAKE-UP

Treaty	Number of parties
Inhumane Weapons Treaty (1981)	32
Antarctic Treaty (1959)	39
Environmental Modification Treaty (1977)	55
Outer Space Treaty (1967)	93
Biological Warfare Treaty (1972)	112
Partial Test Ban Treaty (1963)	119
Geneva Protocol (1925)	125
Non-Proliferation Treaty (1968)	141

NUMBER OF PARTIES PER TREATY *as of 1 January 1990*

GREENLAND
(Den)

ICELAND

C A N A D A

NORWAY

SWEDEN

DENMARK

UNITED
KINGDOM

IRELAND

NETH. GERMANY
West Germany
only

BEL

CZEC

AUS

S

UNITED STATES
OF AMERICA

FRANCE

ITALY

YUG

BERMUDA

PORTUGAL   SPAIN

ATLANTIC
OCEAN

TUNISIA

MOROCCO

MEXICO

BAHAMAS

WESTERN SAHARA

ALGERIA

LIB

CUBA

MAURITANIA

MALI

NIGER

BELIZE   1989-
HONDURAS
GUATEMALA

HAITI
DOMINICAN REPUBLIC
PUERTO RICO (US)

JAMAICA   1965-66

CAPE VERDE

SENEGAL
GAMBIA

EL SALVADOR

DOMINICA
MARTINIQUE (Fr)

GUINEA-BISSAU

GUINEA

BURKINA

NICARAGUA   1989-

BARBADOS

SIERRA LEONE

IVORY
COAST

BENIN
GHANA
TOGO

NIGERIA

COSTA RICA

TRINIDAD & TOBAGO

LIBERIA

PANAMA

VENEZUELA   GUYANA

CAMEROON

SURINAME

FRENCH GUIANA (Fr)

EQUATORIAL GUINEA

SAO TOME & PRINCIPE

GABON

CONGO

COLOMBIA

ECUADOR

PERU

B R A Z I L

PACIFIC
OCEAN

ATLANTIC
OCEAN

ANG

1989-

BOLIVIA

1988-

NAMIB

PARAGUAY

CHILE

URUGUAY

ARGENTINA

FORCE FOR PEACE

STATES CONTRIBUTING
TROOPS AND/OR POLICE OFFICERS
TO MULTILATERAL
PEACEKEEPING FORCES
1989

- 7 or 8 forces
- 5 or 6 forces
- 3 or 4 forces
- 1 or 2 forces
- none

A MITE FOR PEACE

Numbers of troops and percentage
of states' armed forces contributed
to multinational peacekeeping forces
1989

Czechoslovakia 0.004 Panama 0.4
Togo 0.4   Bangladesh 0.02
New Zealand 0.4   Uruguay 0.3   Spain 0.03

Netherlands 0.1

Italy 0.06

Australia 0.5

Denmark 1.4

Colombia 0.4

Fr

percentage

troops

100

500

Sources in notes

The presence of multilateral peacekeeping forces in conflict areas can ensure that ceasefires and peace treaties are respected. In 1989, 54 states contributed about 16,000 troops and police officers to 12 peacekeeping forces.

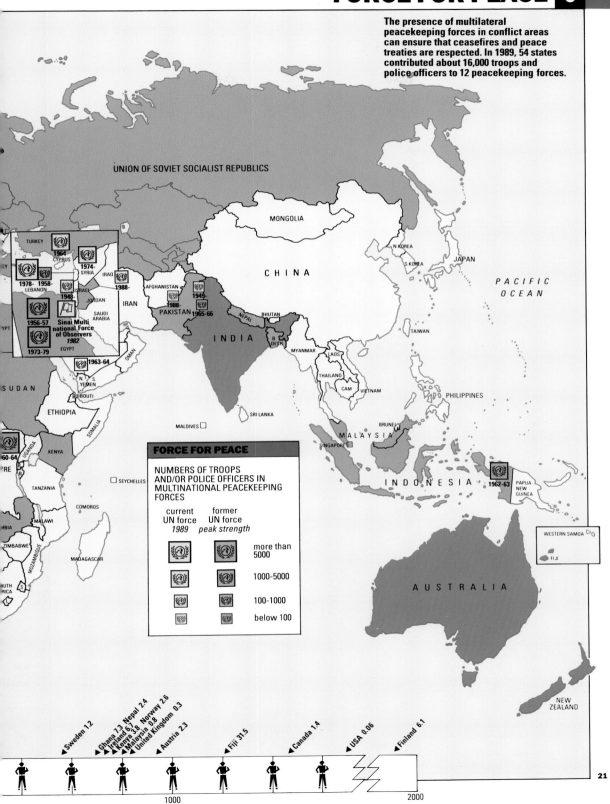

UNION OF SOVIET SOCIALIST REPUBLICS

MONGOLIA

CHINA

TURKEY

1964
CYPRUS

1974-
SYRIA

1978- 1958-
LEBANON

ISRAEL
JORDAN

IRAQ

1988-

AFGHANISTAN

1988-
PAKISTAN

1949-

1965-66

SAUDI
ARABIA

IRAN

1956-57

Sinai Multi
national Force
of Observers
1982

1973-79 EGYPT

1963-64

N S
YEMEN

OMAN

DJIBOUTI

SUDAN

ETHIOPIA

SOMALIA

KENYA

UGANDA

60-64

TANZANIA

COMOROS

MALAWI

MBIA

ZIMBABWE

MOZAMBIQUE

MADAGASCAR

SEYCHELLES

MALDIVES

SRI LANKA

N KOREA

S KOREA

JAPAN

PACIFIC
OCEAN

TAIWAN

INDIA

NEPAL

BHUTAN

B
DESH

MYANMAR

LAOS

THAILAND

CAM

VIETNAM

PHILIPPINES

BRUNEI

MALAYSIA

SINGAPORE

INDONESIA

1962-63

PAPUA
NEW
GUINEA

WESTERN SAMOA

FIJI

AUSTRALIA

NEW
ZEALAND

FORCE FOR PEACE

NUMBERS OF TROOPS
AND/OR POLICE OFFICERS IN
MULTINATIONAL PEACEKEEPING
FORCES

current
UN force
1989

former
UN force
peak strength

more than
5000

1000-5000

100-1000

below 100

Sweden 1.2
Ghana 7.3
Ireland 6.7
Kenya 3.8
Nepal 2.4
Malaysia 0.8
Norway 2.6
United Kingdom 0.3
Austria 2.3
Fiji 31.5
Canada 1.4
USA 0.06
Finland 6.1

1000

2000

GREENLAND
(Den)

ICELAND

CANADA

NORWAY
SWEDEN
DENMARK
UNITED KINGDOM
NETH. GERMANY
IRELAND
1969
BEL
PO
CZECH
AUS
FRANCE
YUGO
SLAVIA
1973
SPAIN
1977
ITALY

UNITED STATES
OF AMERICA

PORTUGAL

ATLANTIC
OCEAN

TUNISIA
MOROCCO
ALGERIA
LIBY

WESTERN
SAHARA
Morocco 1976

BERMUDA

MEXICO

BAHAMAS

CUBA
HAITI

DOMINICAN REPUBLIC
PUERTO RICO (US)

MAURITANIA

MALI
NIGER
19
CH

CAPE VERDE
SENEGAL
GAMBIA
GUINEA-BISSAU
GUINEA

BURKINA

IVORY
COAST
GHANA
BENIN
TOGO
NIGERIA

BELIZE
HONDURAS
USA 1968
GUATEMALA
EL SALVADOR
NICARAGUA
1970
USA
Cuba
COSTA RICA
USA 1979

GUADELOUPE (Fr)
DOMINICA
MARTINIQUE (Fr)
BARBADOS
TRINIDAD & TOBAGO

PANAMA
USA 1989
1986
USA
COLOMBIA
VENEZUELA
GUYANA
SURINAME
FRENCH GUIANA (Fr)
1986

SIERRA LEONE
LIBERIA

1989

CAMEROON
EQUATORIAL GUINEA
GABON
CONGO

ECUADOR

PERU
1980

BRAZIL

PACIFIC
OCEAN

USA 1985
BOLIVIA

CHILE

PARAGUAY

URUGUAY

ARGENTINA

Cuba 19
South Africa
ANGO

NAMIBIA

FALKLAND ISLANDS (Br)

THE DOGS OF WAR

STATES IN WHICH WAR TOOK PLACE
at any time September 1989–August 1990

main conflict with other states.

- general

- limited

main conflict with own citizens:

- general

- limited
  secessionist and/or regional

- other states

1975 first year of war

SIGNIFICANT FOREIGN PRESENCE

combat troops
technical support

In this atlas we have regarded an open armed conflict as war if:
- *regular armed forces are engaged on at least one side;*
- *the fighters and fighting are organized centrally to some extent;*
- *there is some continuity between clashes.*

Sources in notes

There was warfare in 39 states at the turn of the decade, three less than ten years before. The wars were bloodier and more of them were being fought on home soil, against the state's own citizens.

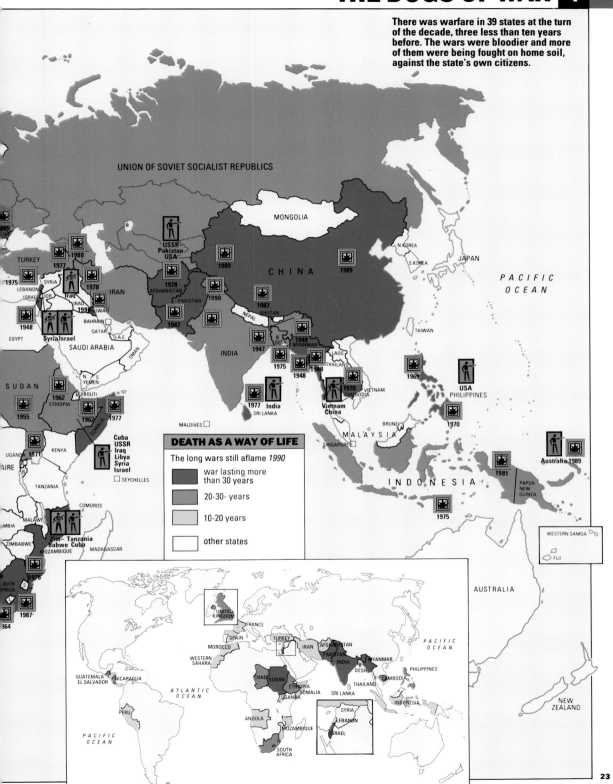

UNION OF SOVIET SOCIALIST REPUBLICS

MONGOLIA

N KOREA

S KOREA

JAPAN

PACIFIC OCEAN

CHINA

USSR
Pakistan
USA

1989

1989

TURKEY

1977

1988

1975

SYRIA

1978

IRAN

1978
AFGHANISTAN

PAKISTAN

1990

1987

BHUTAN

NEPAL

TAIWAN

LEBANON

ISRAEL JOR.

Iraq

IRAQ

1990

KUWAIT

BAHRAIN

1948

Syria Israel

QATAR

U.A.E

EGYPT

SAUDI ARABIA

OMAN

N. S. YEMEN

DJIBOUTI

1947

B DESH

1948
MYANMAR

LAOS

THAILAND

INDIA

1975

1948

1948

VIETNAM

1969

USA
PHILIPPINES

1970

SUDAN

1962
ETHIOPIA

1955

1962

SOMALIA

1977

MALDIVES

1977

India

1970
CAMBODIA

Vietnam
China

SRI LANKA

BRUNEI

MALAYSIA

SINGAPORE

Cuba
USSR
Iraq
Libya
Syria
Israel

SEYCHELLES

UGANDA

1971

KENYA

ZAIRE

TANZANIA

COMOROS

I N D O N E S I A

PAPUA NEW GUINEA

1981

Australia 1989

1975

AIRE

MALAWI

MBIA

ZIMBABWE

Zim-
babwe

Tanzania
Cuba

MOZAMBIQUE

MADAGASCAR

WESTERN SAMOA

FIJI

DEATH AS A WAY OF LIFE

The long wars still aflame *1990*

- war lasting more than 30 years
- 20-30- years
- 10-20 years
- other states

SOUTH AFRICA

1976

1987-

1964

(inset world map)

UNITED KINGDOM

FRANCE

SPAIN

TURKEY

MOROCCO

WESTERN SAHARA

GUATEMALA
EL SALVADOR

NICARAGUA

ATLANTIC OCEAN

PERU

PACIFIC OCEAN

IRAN

AFGHANISTAN

PAKISTAN

INDIA

CHAD

SUDAN

ETHIOPIA

UGANDA

SOMALIA

MYANMAR

B DESH

THAILAND

SRI LANKA

CAMBODIA

PHILIPPINES

INDONESIA

PACIFIC OCEAN

AUSTRALIA

NEW ZEALAND

ANGOLA

MOZAMBIQUE

SOUTH AFRICA

SYRIA

LEBANON

ISRAEL

23

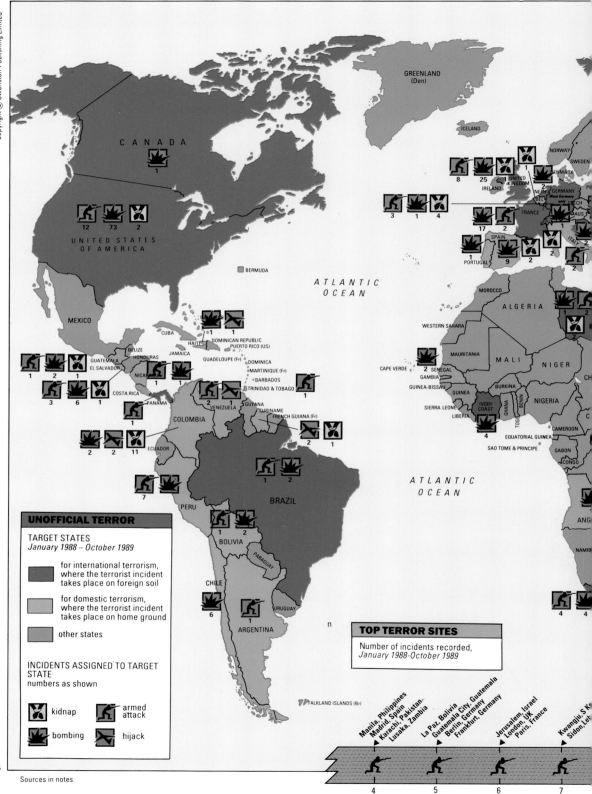

GREENLAND
(Den)

ICELAND

NORWAY

SWEDEN

DENMARK

IRELAND

UNITED
KINGDOM

NETH
BELG

GERMANY
West Germany
only

CZECH

FRANCE

AUS

SWITZ

ITALY

SPAIN

PORTUGAL

C A N A D A

U N I T E D   S T A T E S
O F   A M E R I C A

BERMUDA

A T L A N T I C
O C E A N

MEXICO

CUBA

HAITI

JAMAICA

BELIZE

GUATEMALA

EL SALVADOR

HONDURAS

NICARAGUA

COSTA RICA

PANAMA

DOMINICAN REPUBLIC
PUERTO RICO (US)

GUADELOUPE (Fr)

DOMINICA

MARTINIQUE (Fr)

BARBADOS

TRINIDAD & TOBAGO

VENEZUELA

GUYANA

SURINAME

FRENCH GUIANA (Fr)

COLOMBIA

ECUADOR

PERU

BRAZIL

BOLIVIA

PARAGUAY

CHILE

URUGUAY

ARGENTINA

MOROCCO

WESTERN SAHARA

ALGERIA

MAURITANIA

MALI

NIGER

CAPE VERDE

SENEGAL

GAMBIA

GUINEA-BISSAU

GUINEA

SIERRA LEONE

LIBERIA

IVORY
COAST

GHANA

BURKINA

TOGO

BENIN

NIGERIA

CAMEROON

EQUATORIAL GUINEA

SAO TOME & PRINCIPE

GABON

CONGO

A T L A N T I C
O C E A N

ANG

NAMIB

FALKLAND ISLANDS (Br)

UNOFFICIAL TERROR

TARGET STATES
January 1988 – October 1989

- for international terrorism, where the terrorist incident takes place on foreign soil
- for domestic terrorism, where the terrorist incident takes place on home ground
- other states

INCIDENTS ASSIGNED TO TARGET
STATE
numbers as shown

- kidnap
- bombing
- armed attack
- hijack

TOP TERROR SITES

Number of incidents recorded,
January 1988-October 1989

Manila, Philippines
Madrid, Spain
Karachi, Pakistan
Lusaka, Zambia

La Paz, Bolivia
Guatemala City, Guatemala
Berlin, Germany
Frankfurt, Germany

Jerusalem, Israel
London, UK
Paris, France

Kwangju S K
Sidon, Leb

4   5   6   7

Sources in notes

If war is the pursuit of policies by other means, so is terrorism – a low level, low intensity form of warfare.

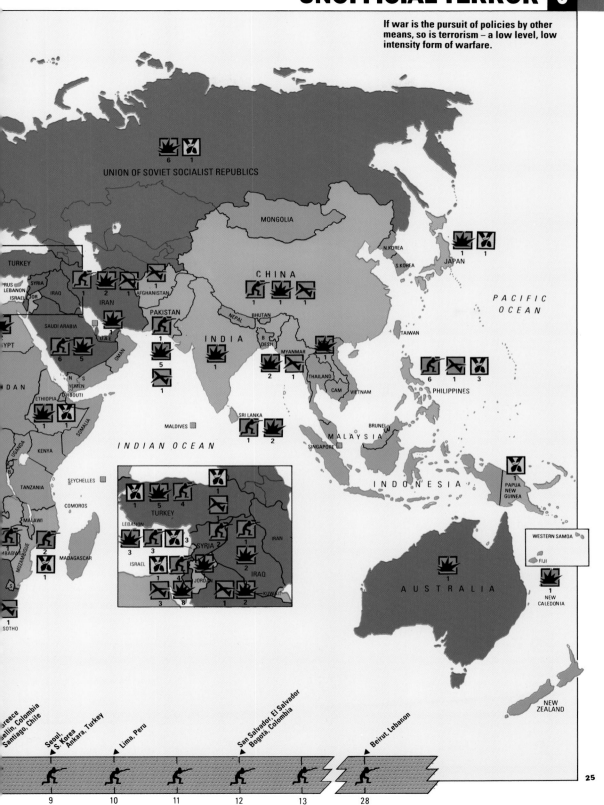

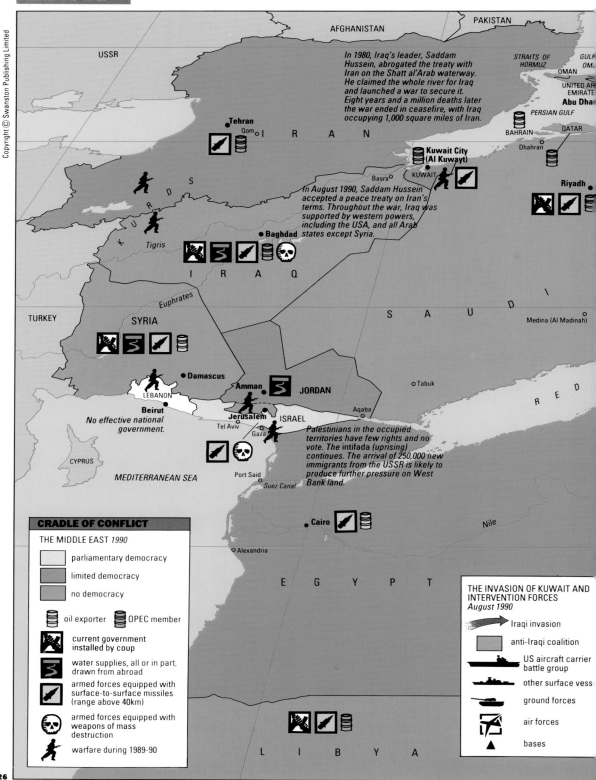

In 1980, Iraq's leader, Saddam Hussein, abrogated the treaty with Iran on the Shatt al'Arab waterway. He claimed the whole river for Iraq and launched a war to secure it. Eight years and a million deaths later the war ended in ceasefire, with Iraq occupying 1,000 square miles of Iran.

In August 1990, Saddam Hussein accepted a peace treaty on Iran's terms. Throughout the war, Iraq was supported by western powers, including the USA, and all Arab states except Syria.

Palestinians in the occupied territories have few rights and no vote. The intifada (uprising) continues. The arrival of 250,000 new immigrants from the USSR is likely to produce further pressure on West Bank land.

LEBANON
No effective national government.

CRADLE OF CONFLICT

THE MIDDLE EAST *1990*

- parliamentary democracy
- limited democracy
- no democracy

oil exporter   OPEC member

current government installed by coup

water supplies, all or in part, drawn from abroad

armed forces equipped with surface-to-surface missiles (range above 40km)

armed forces equipped with weapons of mass destruction

warfare during 1989-90

THE INVASION OF KUWAIT AND INTERVENTION FORCES
August 1990

Iraqi invasion

anti-Iraqi coalition

US aircraft carrier battle group

other surface vess

ground forces

air forces

bases

26

Sources in notes

Copyright © Swanston Publishing Limited

Instability in the Middle East is fed by internal strains, as the powerful few control and squander natural resources at the expense of the impoverished many – as much as by the ambitions of national leaders and conflict between states.

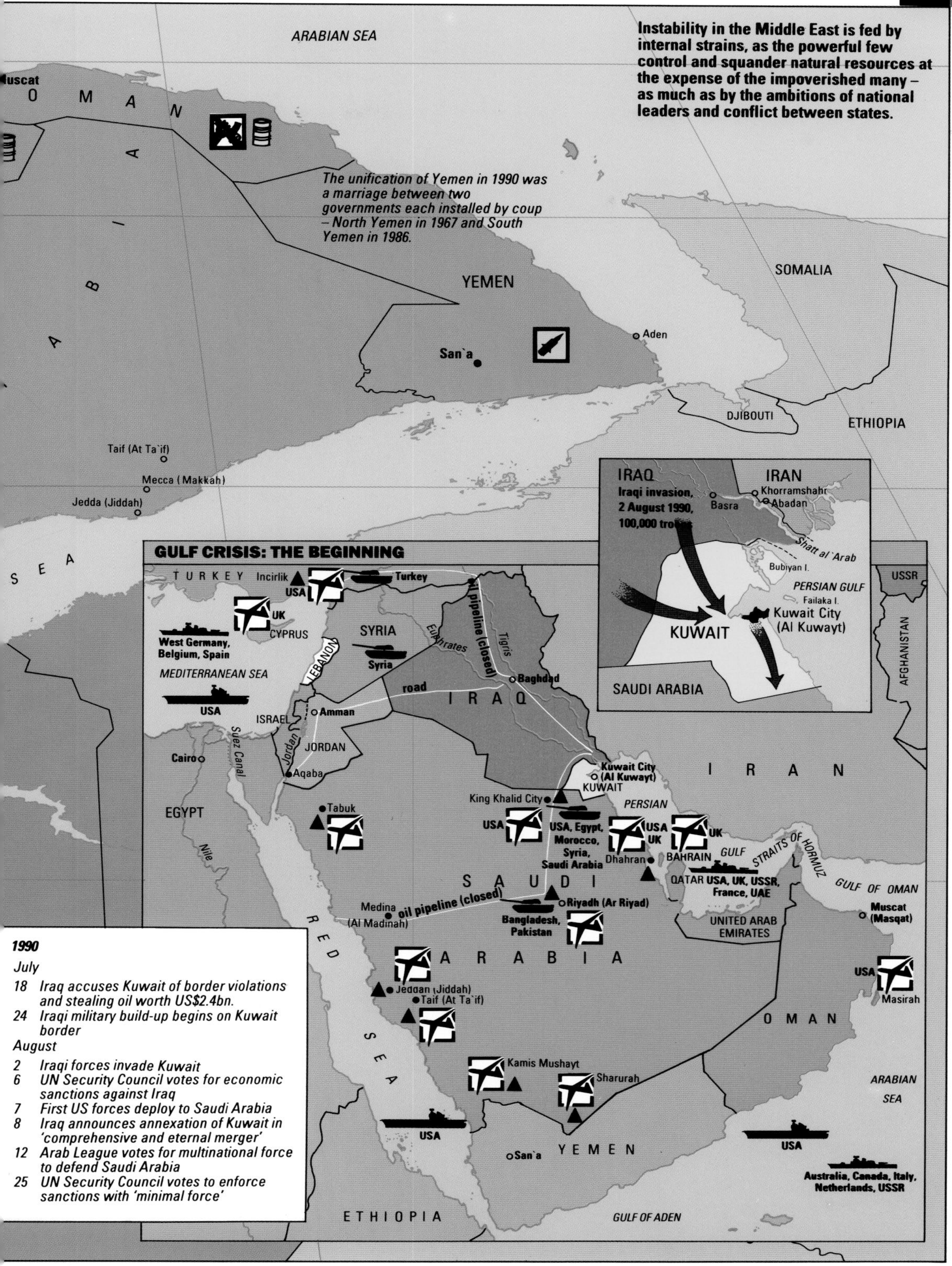
ARABIAN SEA
Muscat
OMAN
ARABIA
SEA
The unification of Yemen in 1990 was a marriage between two governments each installed by coup – North Yemen in 1967 and South Yemen in 1986.
YEMEN
SOMALIA
Aden
San`a
DJIBOUTI
ETHIOPIA
Taif (At Ta`if)
Mecca (Makkah)
Jedda (Jiddah)
IRAQ
Iraqi invasion, 2 August 1990, 100,000 troops
IRAN
Basra
Khorramshahr
Abadan
Shatt al `Arab
Bubiyan I.
PERSIAN GULF
Failaka I.
Kuwait City (Al Kuwayt)
KUWAIT
SAUDI ARABIA
GULF CRISIS: THE BEGINNING
TURKEY
Incirlik
USA
Turkey
USSR
UK
CYPRUS
West Germany, Belgium, Spain
MEDITERRANEAN SEA
USA
SYRIA
Syria
LEBANON
Euphrates
Tigris
oil pipeline (closed)
road
Baghdad
IRAQ
ISRAEL
Amman
JORDAN
Jordan
Suez Canal
Cairo
Aqaba
EGYPT
Nile
Tabuk
Kuwait City (Al Kuwayt)
KUWAIT
King Khalid City
USA
USA, Egypt, Morocco, Syria, Saudi Arabia
USA
UK
UK
PERSIAN GULF
Dhahran
BAHRAIN
STRAITS OF HORMUZ
QATAR USA, UK, USSR, France, UAE
IRAN
AFGHANISTAN
GULF OF OMAN
Muscat (Masqat)
SAUDI ARABIA
Medina (Al Madinah)
oil pipeline (closed)
Riyadh (Ar Riyad)
Bangladesh, Pakistan
UNITED ARAB EMIRATES
RED SEA
Jeddah (Jiddah)
Taif (At Ta`if)
USA
Masirah
OMAN
Kamis Mushayt
Sharurah
ARABIAN SEA
USA
USA
San`a
YEMEN
Australia, Canada, Italy, Netherlands, USSR
ETHIOPIA
GULF OF ADEN

1990

July

18 *Iraq accuses Kuwait of border violations and stealing oil worth US$2.4bn.*

24 *Iraqi military build-up begins on Kuwait border*

August

2 *Iraqi forces invade Kuwait*

6 *UN Security Council votes for economic sanctions against Iraq*

7 *First US forces deploy to Saudi Arabia*

8 *Iraq announces annexation of Kuwait in 'comprehensive and eternal merger'*

12 *Arab League votes for multinational force to defend Saudi Arabia*

25 *UN Security Council votes to enforce sanctions with 'minimal force'*

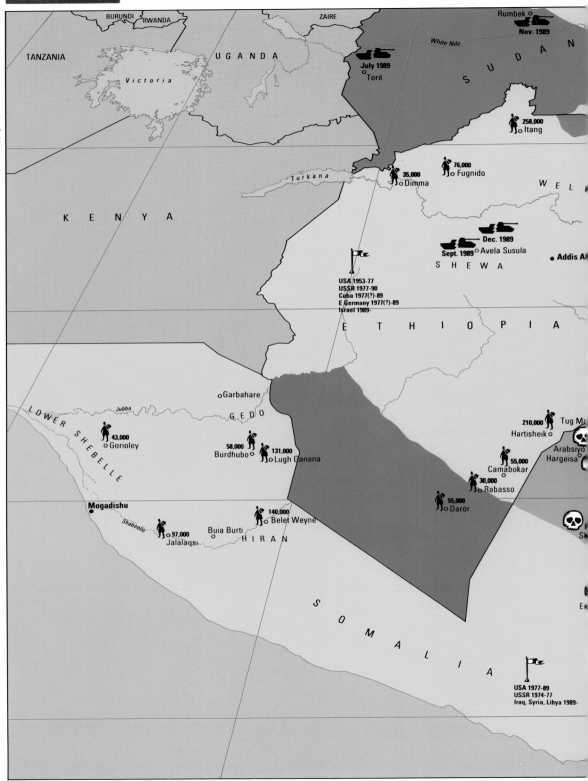

Copyright © Swanston Publishing Limited

BURUNDI RWANDA

ZAIRE

Rumbek o

Nov. 1989

TANZANIA

UGANDA

SUDAN

July 1989
Torit

White Nile

Victoria

258,000
o Itang

Turkana

76,000
o Fugnido

35,000
o Dimma

WEL

KENYA

Dec. 1989
o Avela Susula

Sept. 1989

SHEWA

• Addis A

USA 1953-77
USSR 1977-90
Cuba 1977(?)-89
E Germany 1977(?)-89
Israel 1989-

ETHIOPIA

o Garbahare

GEDO

210,000
Tug M
Hartisheik o

LOWER
SHEBELLE

Jubba

43,000
o Gorioley

Arabsiyo
Hargeisa

58,000
Burdhubo o

131,000
o Lugh Ganana

55,000
Camabokar
o

30,000
o Rabasso

55,000
o Daror

Mogadishu

Shabeelle

140,000
o Belet Weyne

97,000
o
Jalalaqsi

Buia Burti
o

HIRAN

S

O

M

A

L

I

A

E

S

USA 1977-89
USSR 1974-77
Iraq, Syria, Libya 1989-

28

Sources in notes

The Horn of Africa is in an advanced state of disintegration: the mighty world powers have flown, the petty regional powers are circling greedily. Fear, famine, flight and fighting abound.

Talawdi
Oct. 1989

Ed Da'ien   El Lagowa   Wau

Fath el Rakham
2,000

Awad elSid 3,000

Tenedba 3,000

● Khartoum

Wad Medani

El Jebelein   Kosti

Fau 5 4,000

2,000
Kilo 7

Abu Rakham 4,000

ct. 1989
Kumuk

Blue Nile

3,000

Um Gulja

S U D A N

USA 1977-85(?)
USSR 1974-77
Iraq, Syria, Libya 1989-

E G Y P T

Ed Damazin 4,000
El Hawala

Mafaza

16,000   5,000

6,000   3,000   Um Gargur 8,000

Tawawa   Abuda

JAM

13,000
Um Rakoba

El Gedaref 12,000
Kilo 26

Um Ali 11,000
Kashmel Girba

Kassala

20,000

Wad
Sherife 44,000

Wad el Hileau 9,000

Port Sudan

Wad Awad 2,000
Gondar

Tana

T I G R A Y   Karkora
12,000   45,000

Shagarab 1.2.3

Feb. 1990

Asmara   Masawa

ct. 1989
ese

Mekele

R E D   S E A

W O L L O

E
R
I
T
R
E
A

R
E
D

S
E
A

DJIBOUTI
,000   Aisha

Djibouti

Asab

S A U D I   A R A B I A

oma
,000

Berbera
kore

Y E M E N

G
u
l
f

o
f

A
d
e
n

eikh

El Afweyna

THE THORN OF AFRICA

THE HORN OF AFRICA *1990*
Insurgent territory held by:

▨	Eritrean People's Liberation Front
▨	Tigray People's Liberation Front
▨	Somali National Movement
▨	Western Somali Liberation Front
▨	Oromo Liberation Front
▨	Sudan People's Liberation Army
▢	other territory

national government military defeats *July 1989-June 1990*
Feb. 1990

massacre of civilians by government forces *1987- 1990*

refugee camps (internationally recognized) *June 1990 approximate populations*

foreign military assistance *1953-1990*

A N G O L A 1975-88

Z A M B I A

Zambezi

From South Africa

B O T S W A N A

•Windhoek

N A M I B I A 1965-88

Pretoria/Witwatersrand/Vaal
Population *1985* 4.7m

Whites 37%

Coloureds 5%

Asians

Blacks 56%

S   O   U   T   H   A   F

C   A   P   E   P   R   O   V   I   N   C   E

Orange

Orange

ATLANTIC
OCEAN

Greater Cape Town
Population *1985* 1.9m

Coloureds 56%

Whites 28%

Blacks 15%

Asians 1%

○Cape Town

Port Elizabeth/Uitenhage
Population *1985* 660,000

Coloureds 26%

Blacks 46%

Whites 27%

Asians 1%

Uitenhage ○ ● Port Elizabeth

THE	**RISE**	**AND**
segregation	1950 sex; registration by race urban residence	

desegregation	1953 labour bargaining rights
	    transport,
	    toilets, parks, benches, education,
	    political representation
		1976 uprising in Soweto spreads
		1977 UN arms embargo
		1981 labour bargaining rights

1910 Union of South Africa formed	1955 ANC Freedom Charter	1982 sport
1913 landownership segregated	1959 Tribal homelands' set up	1984 some university education
1923 residence	residence	1985 economic sanctions
1948 Nationalist government	1960 Sharpeville massacre	sex, some residence,
1949 marriage	ANC adopts armed struggle	political organization

Sources in notes

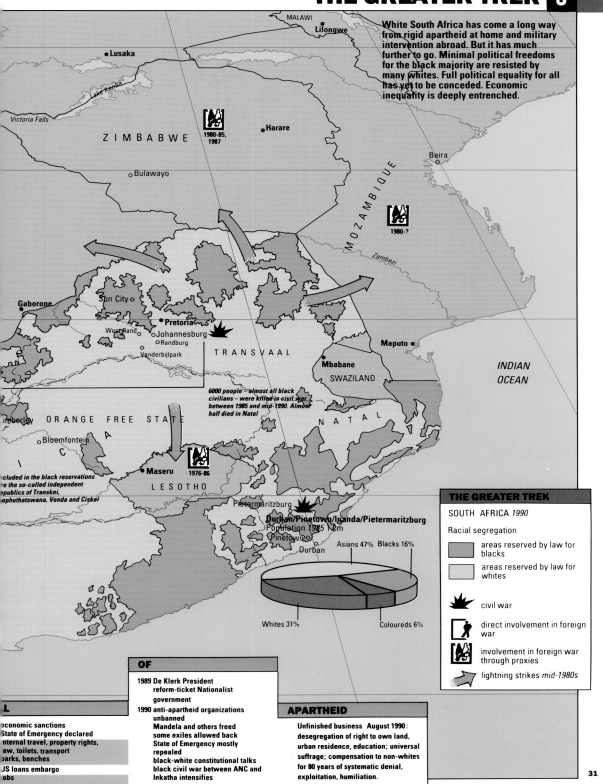

White South Africa has come a long way from rigid apartheid at home and military intervention abroad. But it has much further to go. Minimal political freedoms for the black majority are resisted by many whites. Full political equality for all has yet to be conceded. Economic inequality is deeply entrenched.

MALAWI

Lilongwe

• Lusaka

Lake Kariba

Victoria Falls

ZIMBABWE

1980-85, 1987

• Harare

Beira

○ Bulawayo

MOZAMBIQUE

1980-?

Zambezi

Gaborone

Sun City ○

West Rand

• Pretoria

○ Randburg

○ Johannesburg

Vanderbijlpark

TRANSVAAL

Maputo ●

INDIAN OCEAN

• Mbabane

SWAZILAND

6000 people – almost all black civilians – were killed in civil war between 1985 and mid-1990. Almost half died in Natal

NATAL

imberley

ORANGE FREE STATE

○ Bloemfontein

• Maseru

1976-86

ncluded in the black reservations
re the so-called independent
epublics of Transkei,
ophuthatswana, Venda and Ciskei

LESOTHO

Pietermaritzburg

Durban/Pinetown/Inanda/Pietermaritzburg
Population 1985 1.2m
Pinetown ○
Durban

Pie chart:
- Asians 47%
- Blacks 16%
- Whites 31%
- Coloureds 6%

THE GREATER TREK

SOUTH AFRICA *1990*

Racial segregation

- ▨ areas reserved by law for blacks
- ▨ areas reserved by law for whites
- ✦ civil war
- ▣ direct involvement in foreign war
- ▣ involvement in foreign war through proxies
- ➜ lightning strikes *mid-1980s*

OF

1989 De Klerk President
   reform-ticket Nationalist
   government
1990 anti-apartheid organizations
   unbanned
   Mandela and others freed
   some exiles allowed back
   State of Emergency mostly
   repealed
   black-white constitutional talks
   black civil war between ANC and
   Inkatha intensifies

L

economic sanctions
State of Emergency declared
nternal travel, property rights,
aw, toilets, transport
parks, benches
JS loans embargo
obs

APARTHEID

Unfinished business August 1990:
desegregation of right to own land,
urban residence, education; universal
suffrage; compensation to non-whites
for 80 years of systematic denial,
exploitation, humiliation.

31

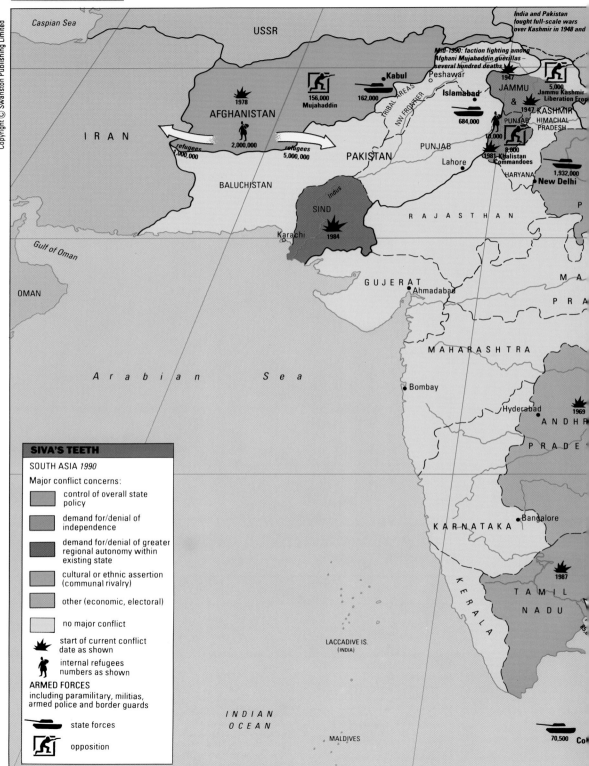

Caspian Sea

USSR

India and Pakistan
fought full-scale wars
over Kashmir in 1948 and

Mid-1990: faction fighting among
Afghani Mujaheddin guerillas –
several hundred deaths

Peshawar

•Kabul

156,000
Mujahaddin

162,000

1978

AFGHANISTAN

Islamabad
•

1947

JAMMU

&

KASHMIR

5,000
Jammu Kashmir
Liberation Front

1947

HIMACHAL
PRADESH

I R A N

684,000

PUNJAB

2,000,000

refugees
1,000,000

refugees
5,000,000

PAKISTAN

PUNJAB

Lahore
•

10,000

9,000
1981 Khalistan
Commandoes

1,932,000

HARYANA

•New Delhi

BALUCHISTAN

Indus

P

SIND

R A J A S T H A N

Karachi•

1984

Gulf of Oman

OMAN

G U J E R A T

•Ahmadabad

M A

P R A

MAHARASHTRA

A r a b i a n   S e a

•Bombay

Hyderabad
•

1969

ANDHR

PRADE

SIVA'S TEETH

SOUTH ASIA *1990*

Major conflict concerns:

- control of overall state
  policy

- demand for/denial of
  independence

- demand for/denial of greater
  regional autonomy within
  existing state

- cultural or ethnic assertion
  (communal rivalry)

- other (economic, electoral)

- no major conflict

- start of current conflict
  date as shown

- internal refugees
  numbers as shown

ARMED FORCES
including paramilitary, militias,
armed police and border guards

- state forces

- opposition

K A R N A T A K A

•Bangalore

K
E
R
A
L
A

1987

T A M I L

N A D U

LACCADIVE IS.
(INDIA)

I N D I A N
O C E A N

MALDIVES

70,500

Co

Ever since the British abandoned their
Indian empire in 1947 the region has been
riven by conflict between, and especially
within, the new states.

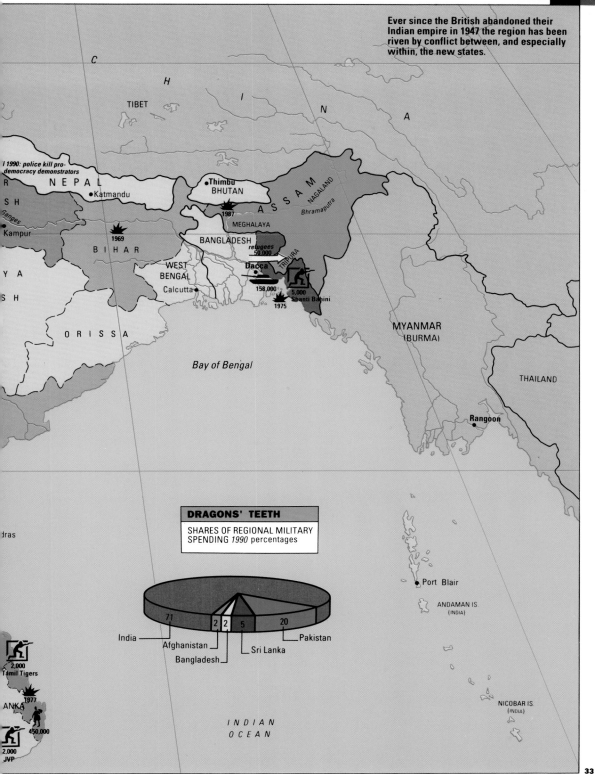

C H I N A

TIBET

1990: police kill pro-
democracy demonstrators

NEPAL

• Katmandu

• Thimbu
BHUTAN

A S S A M

NAGALAND

Bhramaputra

Ganges

1987

MEGHALAYA

• Kampur

1969

BIHAR

BANGLADESH

refugees
50,000

WEST
BENGAL

Dacca

TRIPURA

5,000
Shanti Bahini

Calcutta •

158,000

1975

O R I S S A

MYANMAR
(BURMA)

Bay of Bengal

THAILAND

dras

• Rangoon

DRAGONS' TEETH

SHARES OF REGIONAL MILITARY
SPENDING *1990* percentages

• Port Blair

ANDAMAN IS.
(INDIA)

71

2 2 5

20

India

Afghanistan

Sri Lanka

Pakistan

Bangladesh

2,000
Tamil Tigers

1977

ANKA

450,000

2,000
JVP

NICOBAR IS.
(INDIA)

I N D I A N
O C E A N

C H I N A

Guang
(Canto

INDIA

VIETNAM ● Hanoi

GULF OF
TONGKING

GOLDEN TRIANGLE

MYANMAR
(BURMA)   Mandalay ○

LAOS

● Vientiane

Vietnam 40,000 war dead, 195
1980s; 80,000 refu

Irrawaddi

More than four decades of civil war with
peaks of terror. Death toll 20-40,000.

THAILAND

● Rangoon

ANDAMAN SEA

Bangkok (Krung Thep)
●

CAMBODIA

Vietnam

20 years of war; more than 2 million
350,000 refugees. Vietnamese-back
government faces insurgents includ
forces of Prince Sihanouk (former r
pre-1970) and Khmer Rouge (terroris
government, 1975-78). Peace agree
September 1990.

ARMED FORCES *1989*

👤 forces of state

👤 armed internal opposition

*Vietnam
1,249,000*

*Taiwan
405,500*

*Indonesia
285,000*

*Thailand
283,000*

*Myanmar
200,000*

Malaysia 114,500

Philippines 112,000

Cambodia 99,300

Laos 55,500

Singapore 55,500

25,000   500   2,200   36,500   43,800   60,000   2,000   Brunei 4,200

Joint Thai/Malay operations against
remnants of Malayan Communists, 1!
Communists surrender, December 19
ending more than 40 years of armed
insurrection.

BRUNEI   SABAH

SARAWAK

BORNEO

SULAWESI

I N D O N E S I A

PNG

IRIAN JAYA

J A V A

S U M A T R A

Indonesian invasion of East Timor, 1975;
terror and massacres; over 100,000 killed;
fighting continues.

TIMOR

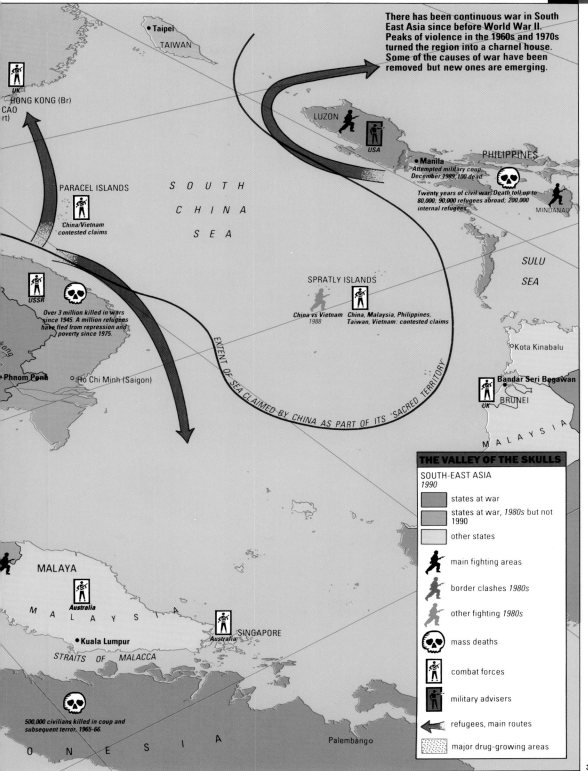

There has been continuous war in South East Asia since before World War II. Peaks of violence in the 1960s and 1970s turned the region into a charnel house. Some of the causes of war have been removed but new ones are emerging.

TAIWAN

• Taipei

UK
HONG KONG (Br)
CAO
rt)

LUZON

USA

PHILIPPINES

• Manila
Attempted military coup,
December 1989, 100 dead

Twenty years of civil war. Death toll up to
80,000; 90,000 refugees abroad; 200,000
internal refugees

MINDANAO

S O U T H

C H I N A

S E A

PARACEL ISLANDS

China/Vietnam
contested claims

SULU

SEA

SPRATLY ISLANDS

China vs Vietnam   China, Malaysia, Philippines,
1988   Taiwan, Vietnam: contested claims

USSR

Over 3 million killed in wars
since 1945. A million refugees
have fled from repression and
poverty since 1975.

Kota Kinabalu

Phnom Penh   ○ Ho Chi Minh (Saigon)

Bandar Seri Begawan

UK
BRUNEI

EXTENT OF SEA CLAIMED BY CHINA AS PART OF ITS "SACRED TERRITORY"

M A L A Y S I A

MALAYA

M A L A Y S I A

Australia

SINGAPORE

Australia

• Kuala Lumpur

STRAITS OF MALACCA

500,000 civilians killed in coup and
subsequent terror, 1965-66.

O   N   E   S   I   A

Palembango

THE VALLEY OF THE SKULLS

SOUTH-EAST ASIA
1990

states at war

states at war, *1980s* but not
1990

other states

main fighting areas

border clashes *1980s*

other fighting *1980s*

mass deaths

combat forces

military advisers

refugees, main routes

major drug-growing areas

Copyright © Swanston Publishing Limited

THE SUPERPOWERS

US AND SOVIET FORCES BASED ABROAD *August 1990*

US	Soviet	
		military bases
		support facilities and/or access for air and naval forces
		space control, monitoring and tracking installations
		electronic intelligence and surveillance stations (including ocean and space surveillance)
		major communications facilities
		early warning radar
		superpower force reductions in progress, impending or under negotiation
		other states

THE HOST STATES

NUMBERS OF SUPERPOWER COMBAT AND SUPPORT FORCES
1989

Italy 15,000
Philippines 17,300
UK 27,900
Poland 40,000
South Korea 43,200
Japan 50,000
Hungary 65,000 *complete withdrawal by mid-1991*
Czechoslovakia 70,000 *complete withdrawal by mid-1991*
West Germany 239,000

Map labels:

CANADA

UNITED STATES OF AMERICA

MEXICO

BERMUDA

BAHAMAS

CUBA

HAITI

BELIZE
GUATEMALA
EL SALVADOR
HONDURAS
NICARAGUA
JAMAICA
COSTA RICA
PANAMA

DOMINICAN REPUBLIC
PUERTO RICO (US)
GUADELOUPE (Fr)
DOMINICA
MARTINIQUE (Fr)
BARBADOS
TRINIDAD & TOBAGO
ANTIGUA & BARBUDA

VENEZUELA
COLOMBIA
GUYANA
SURINAME
FRENCH GUIANA (Fr)
ECUADOR
PERU
BRAZIL
BOLIVIA
PARAGUAY
CHILE
URUGUAY
ARGENTINA

FALKLAND ISLANDS (Br)

ATLANTIC OCEAN

ASCENSION ISLAND (UK)

CAPE VERDE

MOROCCO
WESTERN SAHARA
ALGERIA
TUNISIA
LIB
MAURITANIA
MALI
NIGER
SENEGAL
GAMBIA
GUINEA-BISSAU
GUINEA
SIERRA LEONE
LIBERIA
IVORY COAST
GHANA
TOGO
BENIN
NIGERIA
CAMEROON
EQUATORIAL GUINEA
SAO TOME & PRINCIPE
GABON
CONGO
ANG
NAMI

AZORES (PORTUGAL)

ICELAND
FAEROE ISLANDS
GREENLAND
NORWAY
SWEDEN
FINLAND
IRELAND
UNITED KINGDOM
DENMARK
NETH
GERMANY W E
BEL
LUX
FRANCE
SWITZ
AUSTRIA
POLAND
CZECH.
HUNGARY
ROMA
YUGOSLAVIA
ITALY
ALBANIA
PORTUGAL
GIBRALTAR (Br)
GRE
BU
US

Sources in notes

A global network of superpower bases was put in place during the Cold War.

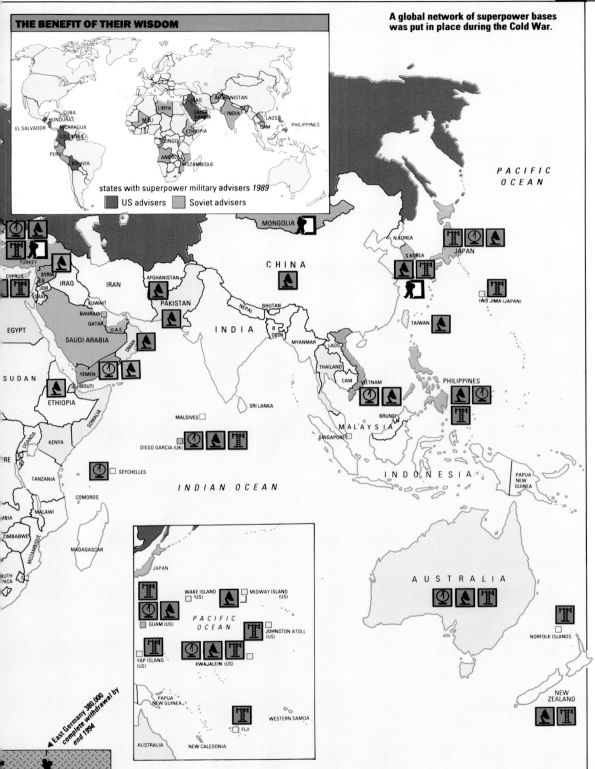

THE BENEFIT OF THEIR WISDOM

CUBA
HONDURAS
EL SALVADOR
NICARAGUA
COLOMBIA
PERU
BOLIVIA

LIBYA
MALI
IRAQ
AFGHANISTAN
SAUDI ARABIA
INDIA
ETHIOPIA
CONGO
ANGOLA
MOZAMBIQUE
LAOS
CAM
PHILIPPINES

states with superpower military advisers 1989

■ US advisers   ■ Soviet advisers

PACIFIC
OCEAN

MONGOLIA

N.KOREA
S.KOREA
JAPAN
IWO JIMA (JAPAN)

TURKEY
CYPRUS
SYRIA
LEB
JOR
ISRAEL
EGYPT
IRAQ
IRAN
AFGHANISTAN
PAKISTAN
KUWAIT
BAHRAIN
QATAR
U.A.E.
SAUDI ARABIA
OMAN
YEMEN
DJIBOUTI

CHINA

NEPAL
BHUTAN
B
DESH

INDIA

MYANMAR
LAOS
THAILAND
CAM
VIETNAM

TAIWAN

PHILIPPINES

BRUNEI

SUDAN
ETHIOPIA
SOMALIA

MALDIVES
SRI LANKA

MALAYSIA
SINGAPORE

UGANDA
KENYA
TANZANIA
COMOROS

DIEGO GARCIA (UK)

SEYCHELLES

INDIAN OCEAN

INDONESIA

PAPUA
NEW
GUINEA

MBIA
MALAWI
ZIMBABWE
MOZAMBIQUE
MADAGASCAR
SOUTH AFRICA

AUSTRALIA

NORFOLK ISLANDS

JAPAN

WAKE ISLAND
(US)
MIDWAY ISLAND
(US)

GUAM (US)

PACIFIC
OCEAN

JOHNSTON ATOLL
(US)

YAP ISLAND
(US)
KWAJALEIN (US)

PAPUA
NEW GUINEA

WESTERN SAMOA

FIJI

AUSTRALIA
NEW CALEDONIA

NEW
ZEALAND

▲ East Germany 380,000
complete withdrawal by
end 1994

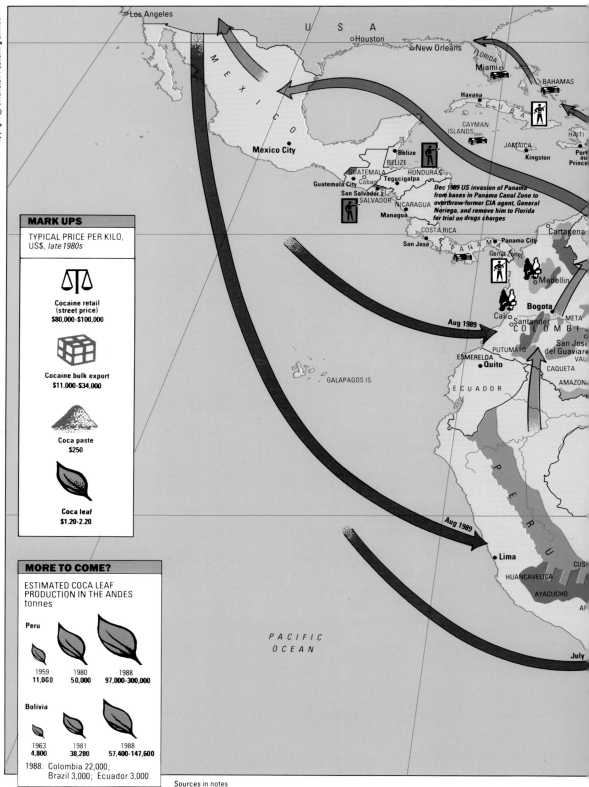

MARK UPS

TYPICAL PRICE PER KILO,
US$, *late 1980s*

**Cocaine retail
(street price)**
$80,000-$100,000

Cocaine bulk export
$11,000-$34,000

Coca paste
$250

Coca leaf
$1.20-2.20

MORE TO COME?

ESTIMATED COCA LEAF
PRODUCTION IN THE ANDES
tonnes

Peru

1959	1980	1988
11,000	**50,000**	**97,000-300,000**

Bolivia

1963	1981	1988
4,800	**38,280**	**57,400-147,600**

1988: Colombia 22,000;
     Brazil 3,000; Ecuador 3,000.

Sources in notes

*Dec 1989 US invasion of Panama
from bases in Panama Canal Zone to
overthrow former CIA agent, General
Noriega, and remove him to Florida
for trial on drugs charges*

Aug 1989

Aug 1989

July

CRACKDOWN 12

Andean coca is a hardy crop with a large and profitable export market. The USA's inability to deal with the drug at home has led it to expand its military role to its South.

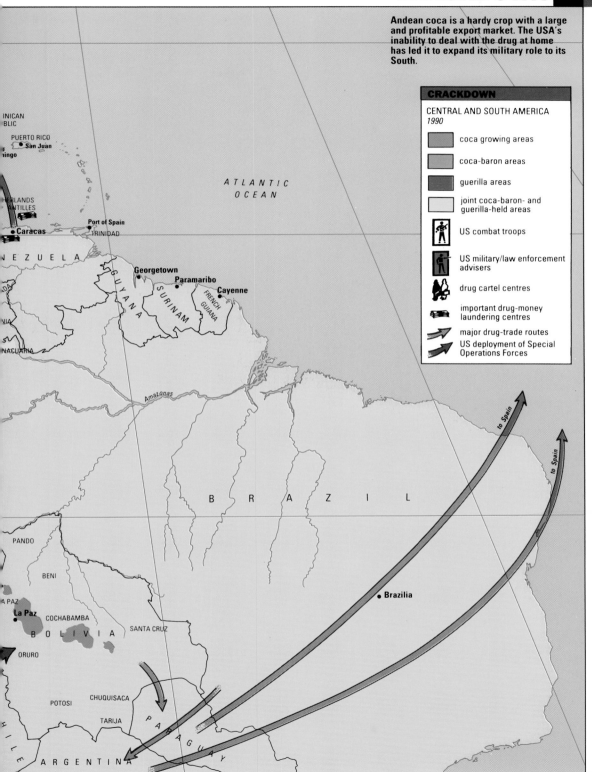

CRACKDOWN

CENTRAL AND SOUTH AMERICA
1990

coca growing areas

coca-baron areas

guerilla areas

joint coca-baron- and guerilla-held areas

US combat troops

US military/law enforcement advisers

drug cartel centres

important drug-money laundering centres

major drug-trade routes

US deployment of Special Operations Forces

ATLANTIC OCEAN

INICAN BLIC

PUERTO RICO
● San Juan
ñingo

HERLANDS ANTILLES

● Caracas

Port of Spain
TRINIDAD

VENEZUELA

GUYANA

Georgetown
●
Paramaribo
●
SURINAM
Cayenne
●
FRENCH GUIANA

NJA

NACUARIA

Amazonas

B R A Z I L

to Spain

to Spain

PANDO

BENI

● Brazilia

A PAZ
La Paz
COCHABAMBA
B O L I V I A
SANTA CRUZ

ORURO

POTOSI
CHUQUISACA

TARIJA
P A R A G U A Y

CHILE

A R G E N T I N A

USSR

MONGOLIA

missile flight path from USSR

missile flight path from USSR

Sovetskaya Gavan

Kamchatka Pen.

Sakhalin

Petropavlovsk

(USSR) (USSR)

(USSR)

Okhabarovsk

Vladivostok

Beijing

Qingdao
(Tsingtao)

(USA)

N KOREA

S KOREA

Kunsan

(USSR)

Yokhta

JAPAN

Yokosaka

CHINA

Shanghai

Sasebo

missile flight pat

NEPAL

BHUTAN

INDIA

BANGLADESH

MYANMAR

LAOS

THAILAND

CAMBODIA

VIETNAM

TAIWAN

HONG KONG (Br)

SOUTH CHINA
SEA

Clark Airbase

Subic Bay

PHILIPPINES

Okinawa

(USA)

missile flight path from China

Iwo Jima

Marcus Island

Wake Island

Saipan

Guam

(USA) (USA)

Eniwetok

Bikini

Yap Island

(USA)

MICRONESIA

MARSHALL
ISLANDS

Kuala Lumpur

MALAYSIA

Singapore

NAURU

INDONESIA

Jakarta

PAPUA
NEW GUINEA

SOLOMON
ISLANDS

INDIAN OCEAN

Darwin

CORAL SEA

VANUATU

New
Caledonia

(UK)

Monte Bello
Islands

AUSTRALIA

(UK)

Maralinga

Brisbane

Norfolk Island

(UK)

Emu

Perth

Sydney

Adelaide

Canberra

Melbourne

TASMAN

SEA

Auckland

*Visits by nuclear-armed ships
banned by New Zealand law since
1985*

Wellingt

NE
ZEALAN

Sources in notes

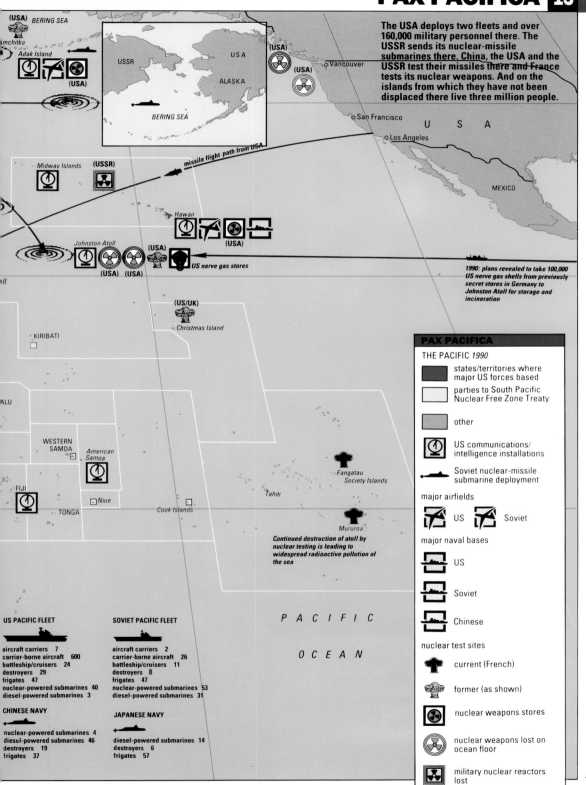

The USA deploys two fleets and over 160,000 military personnel there. The USSR sends its nuclear-missile submarines there. China, the USA and the USSR test their missiles there and France tests its nuclear weapons. And on the islands from which they have not been displaced there live three million people.

(USA) BERING SEA
amchitka
Adak Island
(USA)
(USA)

USSR
USA
ALASKA
BERING SEA

(USA)
(USA)
Vancouver

San Francisco
Los Angeles
U S A
MEXICO

Midway Islands (USSR)
missile flight path from USA

Hawaii
(USA)

Johnston Atoll (USA)
(USA) (USA)
US nerve gas stores

1990: plans revealed to take 100,000 US nerve gas shells from previously secret stores in Germany to Johnston Atoll for storage and incineration

(US/UK)
Christmas Island

KIRIBATI

ALU

WESTERN SAMOA
American Samoa

FIJI
Niue
TONGA
Cook Islands

Tahiti

Fangatau
Society Islands

Mururoa

Continued destruction of atoll by nuclear testing is leading to widespread radioactive pollution of the sea

P A C I F I C

O C E A N

PAX PACIFICA

THE PACIFIC 1990

- states/territories where major US forces based
- parties to South Pacific Nuclear Free Zone Treaty
- other

US communications/ intelligence installations

Soviet nuclear-missile submarine deployment

major airfields
US   Soviet

major naval bases
US
Soviet
Chinese

nuclear test sites
current (French)
former (as shown)
nuclear weapons stores
nuclear weapons lost on ocean floor
military nuclear reactors lost

US PACIFIC FLEET
aircraft carriers 7
carrier-borne aircraft 600
battleship/cruisers 24
destroyers 29
frigates 47
nuclear-powered submarines 40
diesel-powered submarines 3

SOVIET PACIFIC FLEET
aircraft carriers 2
carrier-borne aircraft 26
battleship/cruisers 11
destroyers 8
frigates 47
nuclear-powered submarines 53
diesel-powered submarines 31

CHINESE NAVY
nuclear-powered submarines 4
diesel-powered submarines 46
destroyers 19
frigates 37

JAPANESE NAVY
diesel-powered submarines 14
destroyers 6
frigates 57

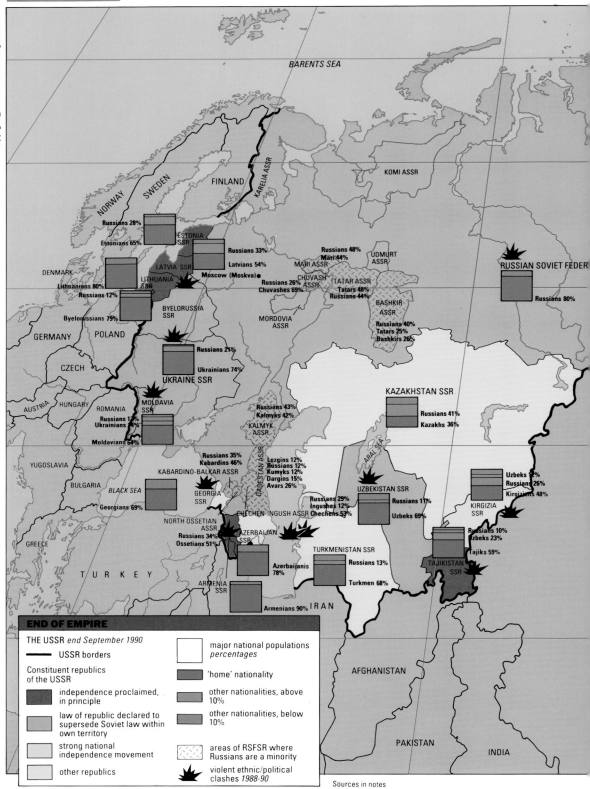

BARENTS SEA

KOMI ASSR

KARELIA ASSR

NORWAY

SWEDEN

FINLAND

RUSSIAN SOVIET FEDER

Russians 28%

Estonians 65%

ESTONIA SSR

Russians 33%

Latvians 54%

LATVIA SSR

Russians 48%
Mari 44%
MARI ASSR

UDMURT ASSR

DENMARK

LITHUANIA SSR

Moscow (Moskva) ●

CHUVASH ASSR

TATAR ASSR

Russians 80%

Lithuanians 80%

Russians 12%

Russians 26%
Chuvashes 69%

Tatars 48%
Russians 44%

BYELORUSSIA SSR

BASHKIR ASSR

Byelorussians 79%

GERMANY

POLAND

MORDOVIA ASSR

Russians 40%
Tatars 25%
Bashkirs 26%

CZECH

Russians 21%

Ukrainians 74%

UKRAINE SSR

KAZAKHSTAN SSR

AUSTRIA   HUNGARY

ROMANIA

MOLDAVIA SSR

Russians 13%
Ukrainians 14%

Moldavians 64%

Russians 43%
Kalmyks 42%

KALMYK ASSR

Russians 41%
Kazakhs 36%

YUGOSLAVIA

Russians 35%
Kabardins 46%

KABARDINO-BALKAR ASSR

Lezgins 12%
Russians 12%
Kumyks 12%
Dargins 15%
Avars 26%

ARAL SEA

Uzbeks 12%
Russians 26%
Kirgizias 48%

BULGARIA

BLACK SEA

GEORGIA SSR

Georgians 69%

DAGESTAN ASSR

CHECHEN-INGUSH ASSR

Russians 29%
Ingushes 12%
Chechens 53%

UZBEKISTAN SSR

Russians 11%

Uzbeks 69%

KIRGIZIA SSR

Russians 10%
Uzbeks 23%

Tajiks 59%

NORTH OSSETIAN ASSR

Russians 34%
Ossetians 51%

AZERBAIJAN SSR

TAJIKISTAN SSR

GREECE

Azerbaijanis 78%

TURKMENISTAN SSR

Russians 13%

Turkmen 68%

T U R K E Y

ARMENIA SSR

Armenians 90%

I R A N

AFGHANISTAN

PAKISTAN

INDIA

END OF EMPIRE

THE USSR *end September 1990*

— USSR borders

Constituent republics of the USSR

	independence proclaimed, in principle
	law of republic declared to supersede Soviet law within own territory
	strong national independence movement
	other republics

major national populations *percentages*

	'home' nationality
	other nationalities, above 10%
	other nationalities, below 10%
	areas of RSFSR where Russians are a minority
	violent ethnic/political clashes *1988-90*

Sources in notes

Gorbachev's programme of reform in the USSR is beset by a sluggish economy, conservative resistance in the Communist Party and, in most of its 15 republics, a rising tide of demands for more independence. The empire which the Bolsheviks inherited from the Tsars in 1917 is nearing the edge of disintegration.

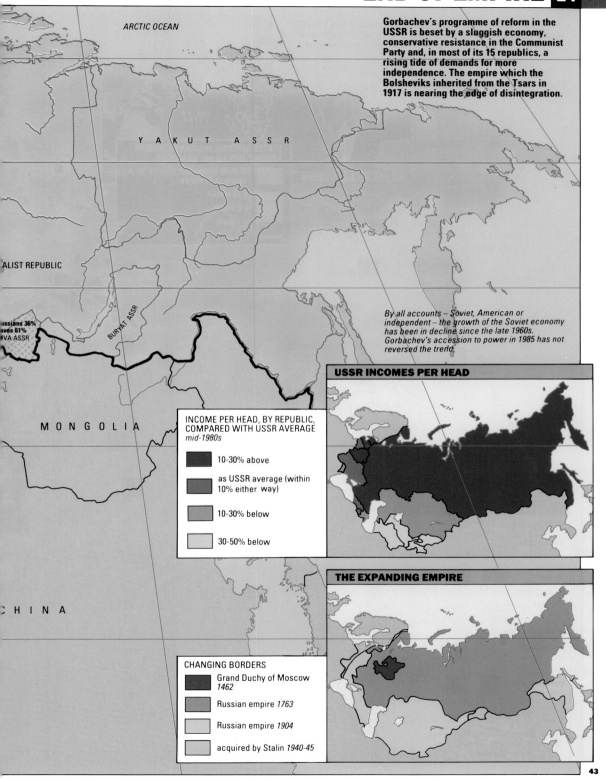

ARCTIC OCEAN

Y A K U T   A S S R

...ALIST REPUBLIC

...ssians 36%
...ves 61%
...VA ASSR

BURYAT ASSR

M O N G O L I A

C H I N A

By all accounts – Soviet, American or independent – the growth of the Soviet economy has been in decline since the late 1960s. Gorbachev's accession to power in 1985 has not reversed the trend.

USSR INCOMES PER HEAD

INCOME PER HEAD, BY REPUBLIC, COMPARED WITH USSR AVERAGE
mid-1980s

- 10-30% above
- as USSR average (within 10% either way)
- 10-30% below
- 30-50% below

THE EXPANDING EMPIRE

CHANGING BORDERS

- Grand Duchy of Moscow *1462*
- Russian empire *1763*
- Russian empire *1904*
- acquired by Stalin *1940-45*

Copyright © Swanston Publishing Limited

ICELAND

FINLAND

NORWAY
SWEDEN

IRELAND
DENMARK
U S

UNITED
KINGDOM
West
Germany

NETH
Belgium
Canada
Netherlands
POLAND

BEL

LUX
GERMANY
late 1990
CZECHOSLOVAKIA

FRANCE
SWITZ
AUSTRIA
HUNGARY
ROMA

ITALY

YUGOSLAVIA
BU

West
Germany
SPAIN
ALBANIA

PORTUGAL
GREE

GIBRALTAR (Br)

C A N A D A

UNITED STATES
OF AMERICA

BERMUDA

MOROCCO
TUNISIA
M

ALGERIA
Ital

WESTERN SAHARA
LIBYA

MEXICO
BAHAMAS

CUBA
ATLANTIC
OCEAN

HAITI
DOMINICAN REPUBLIC
PUERTO RICO (US)

JAMAICA
MAURITANIA
MALI
NIGER

BELIZE
GUADELOUPE (Fr)
DOMINICA
CAPE VERDE

GUATEMALA
HONDURAS
MARTINIQUE (Fr)
SENEGAL

EL SALVADOR
BARBADOS
GAMBIA

NICARAGUA
CURACAO
TRINIDAD & TOBAGO
GUINEA-BISSAU
GUINEA
BURKINA

COSTA RICA
SIERRA- LEONE
IVORY
COAST
GHANA
BENIN
TOGO
NIGERIA

PANAMA
VENEZUELA
GUYANA
LIBERIA

COLOMBIA
SURINAME
FRENCH GUIANA (Fr)
CAMEROON

EQUATORIAL GUINEA

ECUADOR
SAO TOME & PRINCIPE
GABON
CONGO

PERU
B R A Z I L

Morocco

ANC

THE LOCAL POWERS

BOLIVIA

PARAGUAY
NAM

PACIFIC
OCEAN
CHILE

URUGUAY

ARGENTINA

FALKLAND ISLANDS (Br)

FOREIGN MILITARY DEPLOYMENTS
August 1990
numbers of personnel sent abroad
(except USA, USSR, France, Britain
and Cuba)

100,000 or more

10,000-50,000

5000-10,000

1000-5000

less than 1000

other states

expeditionary forces

*Expeditionary forces are those
which are deployed for war, or to
stake a territorial claim, or to exert
decisive influence over the 'host'
state or territory.*

location and origin of :

alliance
forces
(combat)

support groups
and training
camps

46

Sources in notes

In addition to the superpowers and three lesser powers, about 30 states deploy forces outside their borders, mostly confined to their regions.

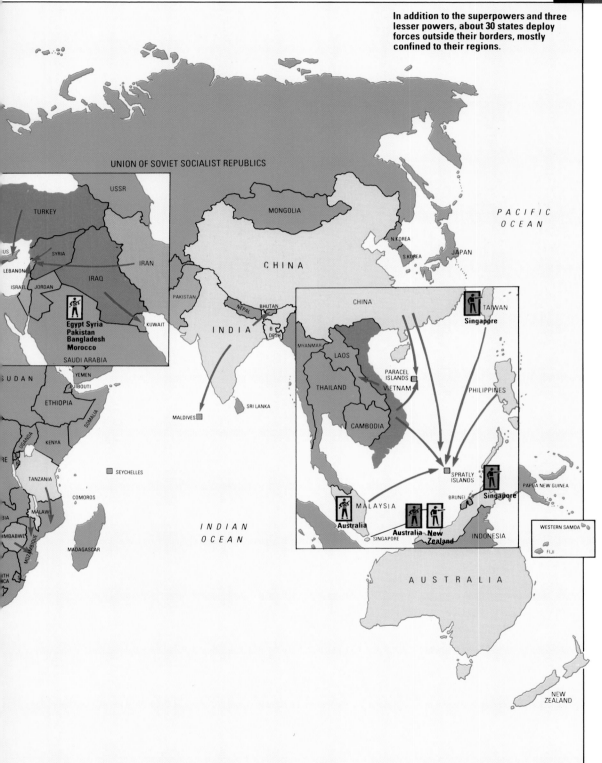

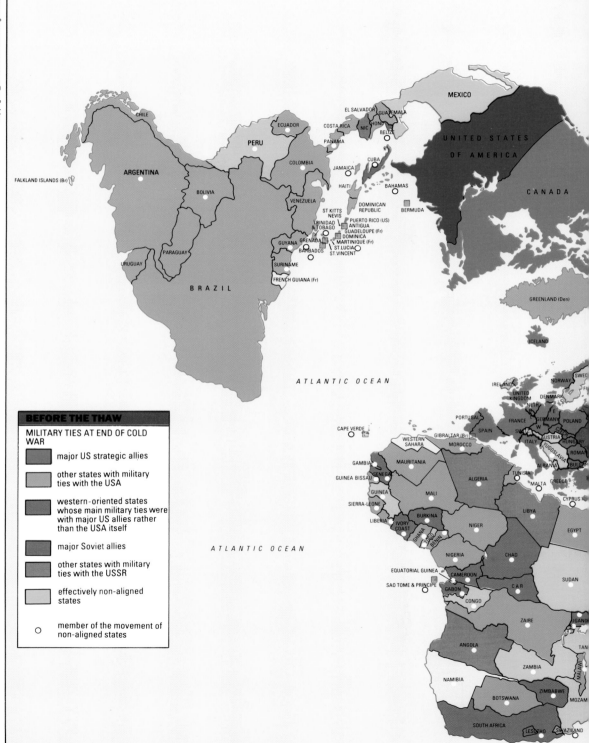

Copyright © Swanston Publishing Limited

CHILE

ECUADOR

PERU

COLOMBIA

ARGENTINA

FALKLAND ISLANDS (Br)

BOLIVIA

VENEZUELA

PARAGUAY

URUGUAY

GUYANA

SURINAME

FRENCH GUIANA (Fr)

BRAZIL

ST KITTS
NEVIS

TRINIDAD
& TOBAGO

GRENADA

BARBADOS

ANTIGUA

GUADELOUPE (Fr)

DOMINICA

MARTINIQUE (Fr)

ST.LUCIA

ST.VINCENT

PUERTO RICO (US)

EL SALVADOR

GUATEMALA

HOND

NIC

BELIZE

COSTA RICA

PANAMA

JAMAICA

CUBA

HAITI

DOMINICAN
REPUBLIC

BAHAMAS

BERMUDA

MEXICO

UNITED STATES
OF AMERICA

CANADA

GREENLAND (Den)

ICELAND

ATLANTIC OCEAN

IRELAND

UNITED
KINGDOM

NORWAY

SWED

FI

DENMARK

NETH

PORTUGAL

SPAIN

FRANCE

GERMANY

POLAND

SW

A

IT

AUSTRIA

HUNGARY

ITALY

YUGOSLAVIA

ROMA

ALBANIA

BULGA

MALTA

GREECE

CYPRUS

GIBRALTAR (Br)

MOROCCO

WESTERN
SAHARA

CAPE VERDE

GAMBIA

GUINEA BISSAU

GUINEA

SIERRA LEONE

LIBERIA

SENEGAL

MAURITANIA

ALGERIA

TUNISIA

LIBYA

EGYPT

MALI

NIGER

CHAD

SUDAN

IVORY
COAST

GHANA

TOGO

BENIN

BURKINA

NIGERIA

CAMEROON

C.A.R.

EQUATORIAL GUINEA

SAO TOME & PRINCIPE

GABON

CONGO

ZAIRE

UGAND

B

TAN

ANGOLA

ZAMBIA

MALAWI

NAMIBIA

BOTSWANA

ZIMBABWE

MOZAM

SOUTH AFRICA

LESOTHO

SWAZILAND

ATLANTIC OCEAN

BEFORE THE THAW

MILITARY TIES AT END OF COLD
WAR

major US strategic allies

other states with military
ties with the USA

western-oriented states
whose main military ties were
with major US allies rather
than the USA itself

major Soviet allies

other states with military
ties with the USSR

effectively non-aligned
states

○ member of the movement of
non-aligned states

Sources in notes

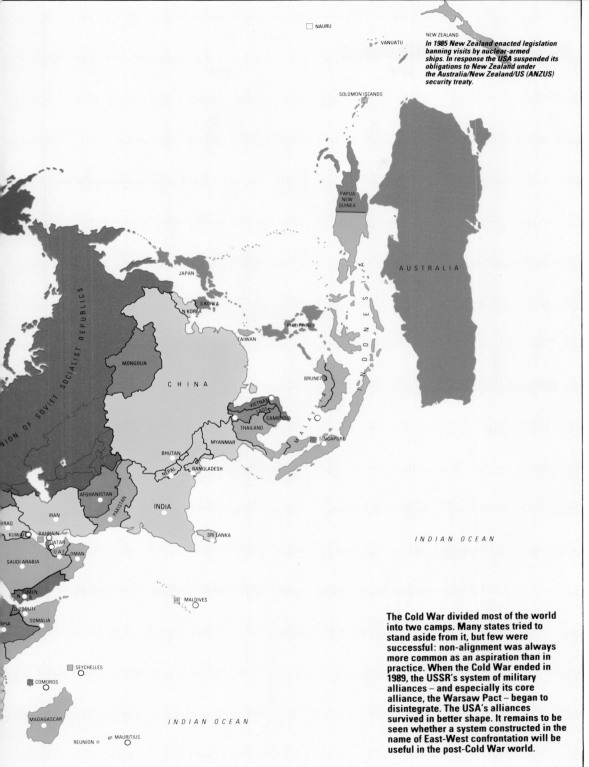

NAURU

NEW ZEALAND

VANUATU

In 1985 New Zealand enacted legislation banning visits by nuclear-armed ships. In response the USA suspended its obligations to New Zealand under the Australia/New Zealand/US (ANZUS) security treaty.

SOLOMON ISLANDS

PAPUA NEW GUINEA

AUSTRALIA

JAPAN

S KOREA
N KOREA

MONGOLIA

TAIWAN

PHILIPPINES

UNION OF SOVIET SOCIALIST REPUBLICS

CHINA

BRUNEI

VIETNAM
LAOS
CAMBODIA
THAILAND

MALAYSIA

INDONESIA

SINGAPORE

BHUTAN
NEPAL BANGLADESH
MYANMAR

AFGHANISTAN
PAKISTAN

IRAN

INDIA

IRAQ
KUWAIT
BAHRAIN
QATAR
U.A.E. OMAN
SAUDI ARABIA

SRI LANKA

INDIAN OCEAN

YEMEN
N
S
DJIBOUTI
PIA SOMALIA

MALDIVES

SEYCHELLES

COMOROS

MADAGASCAR

INDIAN OCEAN

REUNION MAURITIUS

The Cold War divided most of the world into two camps. Many states tried to stand aside from it, but few were successful: non-alignment was always more common as an aspiration than in practice. When the Cold War ended in 1989, the USSR's system of military alliances – and especially its core alliance, the Warsaw Pact – began to disintegrate. The USA's alliances survived in better shape. It remains to be seen whether a system constructed in the name of East-West confrontation will be useful in the post-Cold War world.

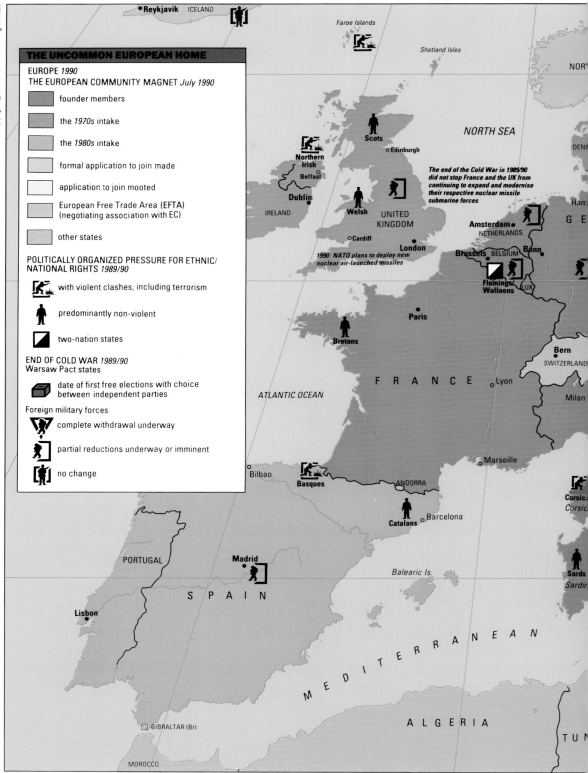

THE UNCOMMON EUROPEAN HOME

EUROPE *1990*
THE EUROPEAN COMMUNITY MAGNET *July 1990*

founder members

the *1970s* intake

the *1980s* intake

formal application to join made

application to join mooted

European Free Trade Area (EFTA)
(negotiating association with EC)

other states

POLITICALLY ORGANIZED PRESSURE FOR ETHNIC/
NATIONAL RIGHTS *1989/90*

with violent clashes, including terrorism

predominantly non-violent

two-nation states

END OF COLD WAR *1989/90*
Warsaw Pact states

date of first free elections with choice
between independent parties

Foreign military forces

complete withdrawal underway

partial reductions underway or imminent

no change

*The end of the Cold War in 1989/90
did not stop France and the UK from
continuing to expand and modernise
their respective nuclear missile
submarine forces*

*1990: NATO plans to deploy new
nuclear air-launched missiles*

Reykjavik ICELAND

Faroe Islands

Shetland Isles

NOR

NORTH SEA

DEN

Scots

Edinburgh

Ham

Northern
Irish
Belfast

GE

Dublin

Welsh

Amsterdam
NETHERLANDS

IRELAND

UNITED
KINGDOM

Cardiff

London

Brussels BELGIUM

Bonn

Flemings/
Walloons LUX

Paris

Bern
SWITZERLAND

Bretons

F R A N C E

Lyon

ATLANTIC OCEAN

Milan

Marseille

Bilbao

Basques

ANDORRA

Corsica
Corsic

Catalans

Barcelona

Sards
Sardi

Madrid

PORTUGAL

Balearic Is.

S P A I N

Lisbon

M E D I T E R R A N E A N

GIBRALTAR (Br)

ALGERIA

TUN

MOROCCO

Sources in notes

With the end of the Cold War in Europe, new problems top the agenda. States are caught between the conflicting pressures of the supra-national economy and the rights demanded by ethnic and national groups.

FINLAND

SWEDEN

Swedes

Helsinki

• Stockholm

Tallin

ESTONIA

Leningrad

BALTIC SEA

LATVIA

Riga

• Copenhagen

LITHUANIA

U   S   S   R

RSFSR

Vilnius

• Moscow

Gdansk

Minsk

BYELORUSSIA

RUSSIAN SOVIET FEDERATED
SOCIALIST REPUBLIC

*East Germany became EC member
as part of Germany upon unification*

POLAND

June
1989

A N Y.

Berlin

Warsaw

Byelorussians

March 1990

Prague Silesians

CZECHOSLOVAKIA

June 1990

UKRAINE

nich

Czechs/
Slovaks

Vienna

Moravians

AUSTRIA

HUNGARY • Budapest

Hungarians

MOLDAVIA

Odessa

May 1990

Slovenes
April/May 1990

March
1990

ROMANIA

South
Tyroleans

SLOVENIA

CROATIA

*1990: violent clashes, supporters of
post-Ceausescu government attack
its critics*

Croats April/May 1990

BOSNIA-
HERZEGOVINA

Nov 1990

SERBIA

Belgrade

Bucharest •

BLACK   SEA

YUGOSLAVIA

Dec 1990

Sofia

June 1990

Albanians

BULGARIA

Turks

O

Rome

ITALY

Pamaks

Istanbul

Nov 1990

Macedonians

Ankara

• Tirana

MACEDONIA

o Naples

ALBANIA

*1989-90: sporadic demonstrations,
police shootings, exodus*

TURKEY

GREECE

Turks

Central & Eastern
Europe 16%

Other 1%

W Germany
18%

Athens

Kurds

EFTA 15%

France 14%

Sicily

E A

• Valletta

MALTA

Other EC 15%

UK 13%

Italy 13%

CYPRUS

north

Nicosia

south

SLICES OF THE PIE

Shares of Europe's income *1989-90*

Greeks/
Turks

Crete

51

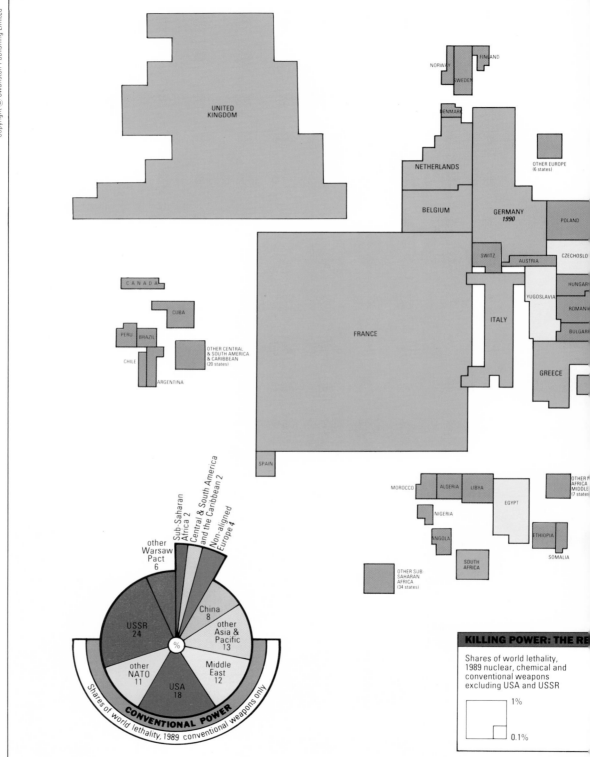

UNITED
KINGDOM

NORWAY

FINLAND

SWEDEN

DENMARK

NETHERLANDS

OTHER EUROPE
(6 states)

BELGIUM

GERMANY
1990

POLAND

SWITZ

AUSTRIA

CZECHOSLO

CANADA

HUNGARY

CUBA

YUGOSLAVIA

ROMANIA

ITALY

PERU

BRAZIL

BULGARI

CHILE

FRANCE

OTHER CENTRAL
& SOUTH AMERICA
& CARIBBEAN
(20 states)

GREECE

ARGENTINA

SPAIN

MOROCCO

ALGERIA

LIBYA

OTHER M
AFRICA
MIDDLE
(7 states)

EGYPT

NIGERIA

ANGOLA

ETHIOPIA

SOUTH
AFRICA

SOMALIA

OTHER SUB-
SAHARAN
AFRICA
(34 states)

Sub-Saharan Africa 2
Central & South America and the Caribbean 2
Non-aligned Europe 4

other
Warsaw
Pact
6

China
8

other
Asia &
Pacific
13

USSR
24

%

Middle
East
12

other
NATO
11

USA
18

CONVENTIONAL POWER

Shares of world lethality, 1989 conventional weapons only

KILLING POWER: THE RE

Shares of world lethality,
1989 nuclear, chemical and
conventional weapons
excluding USA and USSR

1%

0.1%

KILLING POWER: THE SUPERPOWERS AND THE REST

Shares of world lethality nuclear, chemical and conventional weapons *1989*

☐┐ reduction in lethality if US–Soviet Strategic Arms
   Reduction Treaty is agreed

USA 41%

13%

rest of the world 2%

USSR 57%

17%

The USSR and the USA possess almost all of the world's destructive capacity. But many other states can inflict death on a large scale.

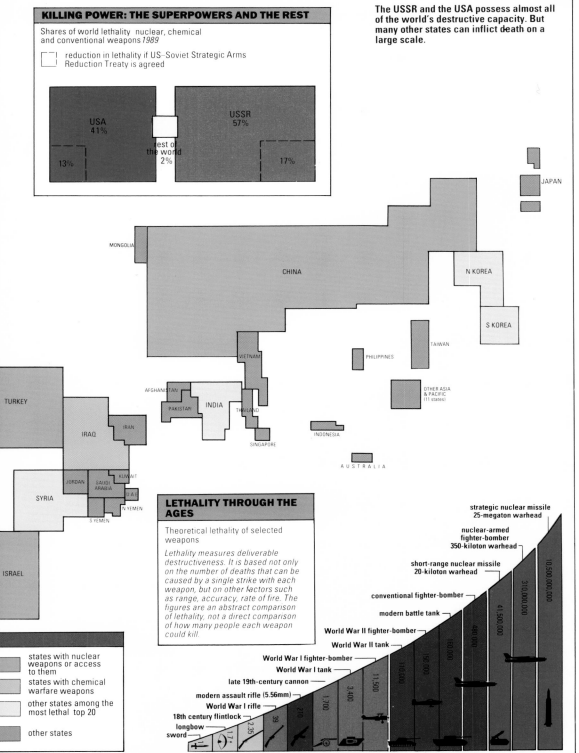

MONGOLIA

CHINA

N KOREA

S KOREA

TAIWAN

VIETNAM

PHILIPPINES

AFGHANISTAN

TURKEY

PAKISTAN

INDIA

THAILAND

OTHER ASIA & PACIFIC (11 states)

IRAQ

IRAN

SINGAPORE

INDONESIA

AUSTRALIA

JORDAN

KUWAIT

SYRIA

SAUDI ARABIA

U.A.E.

N YEMEN

S YEMEN

ISRAEL

JAPAN

LETHALITY THROUGH THE AGES

Theoretical lethality of selected weapons

Lethality measures deliverable destructiveness. It is based not only on the number of deaths that can be caused by a single strike with each weapon, but on other factors such as range, accuracy, rate of fire. The figures are an abstract comparison of lethality, not a direct comparison of how many people each weapon could kill.

strategic nuclear missile 25-megaton warhead — 10,500,000,000

nuclear-armed fighter-bomber 350-kiloton warhead — 310,000,000

short-range nuclear missile 20-kiloton warhead — 41,500,000

conventional fighter-bomber — 480,000

modern battle tank — 180,000

World War II fighter-bomber — 190,000

World War II tank — 116,000

World War I fighter-bomber — 11,500

World War I tank — 3,400

late 19th-century cannon — 1,700

modern assault rifle (5.56mm) — 210

World War I rifle — 39

18th century flintlock — 2.35

longbow — 1.7

sword

states with nuclear weapons or access to them

states with chemical warfare weapons

other states among the most lethal top 20

other states

GREENLAND
(Den)

ICELAND

NORWAY

SWEDEN

C A N A D A

DENMARK

IRELAND

UNITED
KINGDOM

GERMANY

NETH
BEL

CZEC

FRANCE

AUS

UNITED STATES
OF AMERICA

PORTUGAL SPAIN

ITALY

YUGO

BERMUDA

A T L A N T I C
O C E A N

MOROCCO

TUNISIA

A L G E R I A

LIB

MEXICO

BAHAMAS

WESTERN SAHARA

CUBA

DOMINICAN REPUBLIC
PUERTO RICO (US)

MAURITANIA

M A L I

N I G E R

BELIZE
HONDURAS

HAITI

JAMAICA

GUATEMALA
EL SALVADOR

GUADELOUPE (Fr)

DOMINICA

CAPE VERDE

SENEGAL
GAMBIA

C

NICARAGUA

MARTINIQUE (Fr)

GUINEA-BISSAU

BURKINA

COSTA RICA

BARBADOS

TRINIDAD & TOBAGO

GUINEA

IVORY
COAST

GHANA

BENIN

NIGERIA

PANAMA

VENEZUELA

GUYANA

SURINAME

SIERRA LEONE

LIBERIA

TOGO

COLOMBIA

FRENCH GUIANA (Fr)

CAMEROON

ECUADOR

EQUATORIAL GUINEA

SAO TOME & PRINCIPE

GABON

PERU

B R A Z I L

CONGO

A T L A N T I C
O C E A N

ANG

BOLIVIA

NAMI

PARAGUAY

CHILE

THE KILLING FIELDS

WAR SPACE AS A MULTIPLE
OF THE BIOSPHERE *1990*

URUGUAY

ARGENTINA

2600 times

10 times

the same

one-tenth

one-thousandth

WAR SPACE 1990

Million cubic metres

*War space is the space in which the
military routinely operates. It
envelops the world and penetrates
its surface. The biosphere is the
space in which life of any sort can
exist.*

FALKLAND ISLANDS (Br)

▲ Nauru 0.006

▲ Netherlands 130

▲ Sweden 150

▲ Germany 160

▲ Pakistan 170

▲ South Africa 180

▲ Australia 230

▲ Japan 260

▲ China 800

Sources in notes

No fewer than nine states command war spaces larger than the earth's entire life-supporting region. The USSR and the USA each has war space more than 2600 times the volume of the biosphere. For the biocide states the cost of staking out war space has fallen astonishingly in the last 50 years.

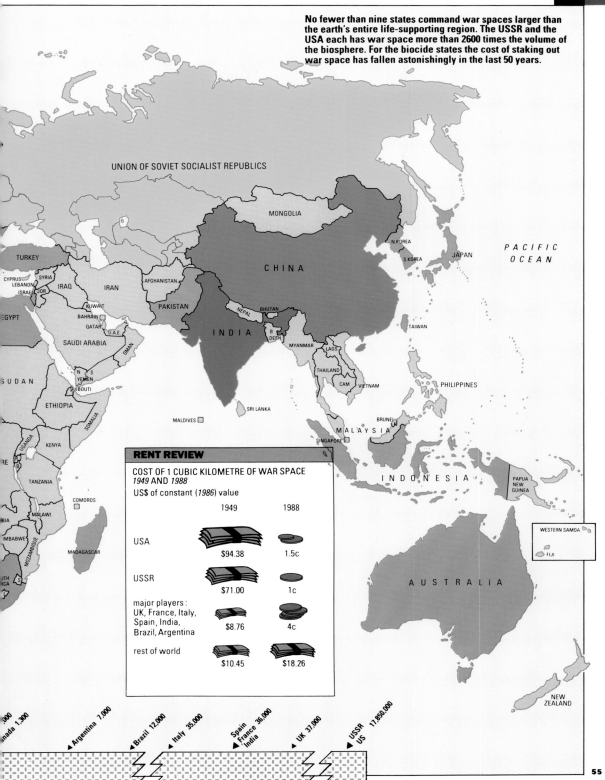

UNION OF SOVIET SOCIALIST REPUBLICS

MONGOLIA

N.KOREA

S.KOREA

JAPAN

PACIFIC OCEAN

TURKEY

CYPRUS
LEBANON
ISRAEL JOR
SYRIA
IRAQ
IRAN
AFGHANISTAN

KUWAIT
BAHRAIN
QATAR
U.A.E.
EGYPT
SAUDI ARABIA
OMAN

PAKISTAN

CHINA

NEPAL BHUTAN

INDIA

B DESH

MYANMAR

LAOS

TAIWAN

THAILAND

CAM VIETNAM

PHILIPPINES

SUDAN

N S
YEMEN
DJIBOUTI

ETHIOPIA

SOMALIA

SRI LANKA

MALDIVES

BRUNEI

MALAYSIA

SINGAPORE

UGANDA
KENYA

TANZANIA

COMOROS

INDONESIA

PAPUA NEW GUINEA

MALAWI

ZIMBABWE

MOZAMBIQUE

MADAGASCAR

AUSTRALIA

WESTERN SAMOA

FIJI

RENT REVIEW

COST OF 1 CUBIC KILOMETRE OF WAR SPACE
1949 AND *1988*
US$ of constant (*1986*) value

	1949	1988
USA	$94.38	1.5c
USSR	$71.00	1c
major players: UK, France, Italy, Spain, India, Brazil, Argentina	$8.76	4c
rest of world	$10.45	$18.26

NEW ZEALAND

▲ Argentina 7,000   ▲ Brazil 12,000   ▲ Italy 35,000   Spain France 36,000 ▲ India   ▲ UK 37,000   ▲ USSR 17,950,000 US

anada 1,300

Copyright © Swanston Publishing Limited

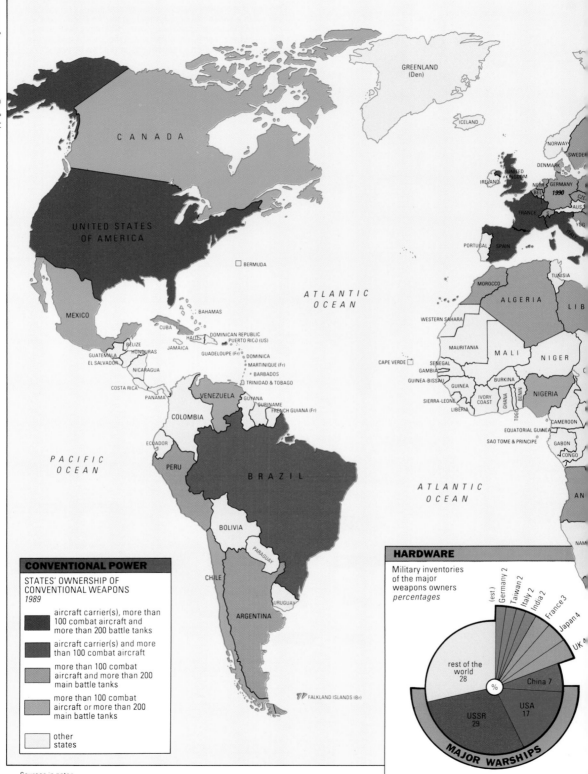

C A N A D A

GREENLAND
(Den)

ICELAND

NORWAY

SWEDE

UNITED STATES
OF AMERICA

UNITED
KINGDOM

DENMARK

IRELAND

NETH GERMANY

BEL

1990

FRANCE

CZE

AUS

YUG

BERMUDA

PORTUGAL

SPAIN

ITALY

MEXICO

BAHAMAS

CUBA

HAITI

DOMINICAN REPUBLIC

PUERTO RICO (US)

BELIZE

HONDURAS

JAMAICA

GUATEMALA

EL SALVADOR

NICARAGUA

GUADELOUPE (Fr)

DOMINICA

MARTINIQUE (Fr)

BARBADOS

TRINIDAD & TOBAGO

COSTA RICA

PANAMA

VENEZUELA

GUYANA

SURINAME

FRENCH GUIANA (Fr)

COLOMBIA

ECUADOR

PERU

B R A Z I L

BOLIVIA

PARAGUAY

CHILE

URUGUAY

ARGENTINA

A T L A N T I C
O C E A N

P A C I F I C
O C E A N

A T L A N T I C
O C E A N

TUNISIA

MOROCCO

ALGERIA

LIB

WESTERN SAHARA

MAURITANIA

M A L I

N I G E R

CAPE VERDE

SENEGAL

GAMBIA

GUINEA-BISSAU

GUINEA

BURKINA

SIERRA LEONE

IVORY
COAST

GHANA

TOGO

BENIN

NIGERIA

LIBERIA

CAMEROON

EQUATORIAL GUINEA

SAO TOME & PRINCIPE

GABON

CONGO

AN

NAM

FALKLAND ISLANDS (Br)

CONVENTIONAL POWER

STATES' OWNERSHIP OF
CONVENTIONAL WEAPONS
1989

aircraft carrier(s), more than
100 combat aircraft and
more than 200 battle tanks

aircraft carrier(s) and more
than 100 combat aircraft

more than 100 combat
aircraft and more than 200
main battle tanks

more than 100 combat
aircraft or more than 200
main battle tanks

other
states

HARDWARE

Military inventories
of the major
weapons owners
percentages

(est)

Germany 2

Taiwan 2

Italy 2

India 2

France 3

Japan 4

UK 4

rest of the
world
28

China 7

%

USSR
29

USA
17

MAJOR WARSHIPS

Sources in notes

There are more than 150,000 main battle tanks, over 40,000 combat aircraft and approximately 2000 major warships worldwide. Ownership is concentrated in a few hands, but several Third World states now have extensive arsenals.

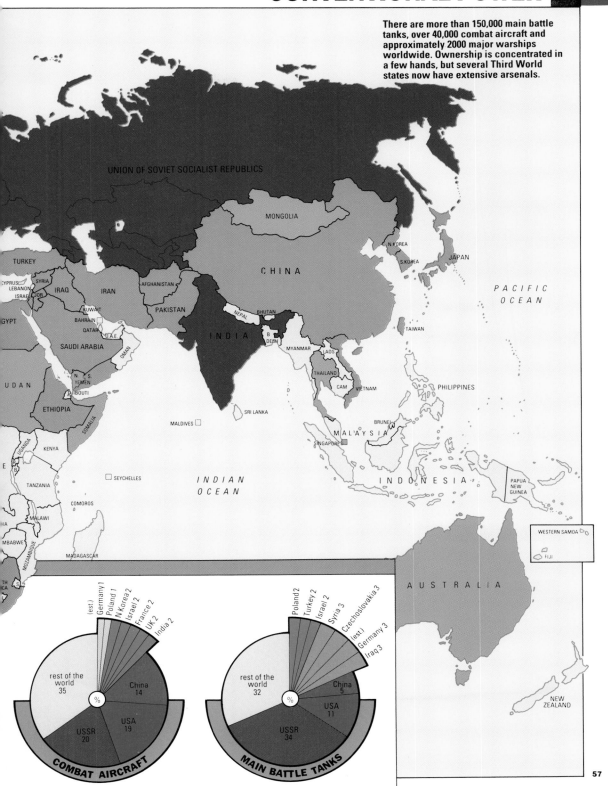

COMBAT AIRCRAFT

rest of the world 35
China 14
USA 19
USSR 20

(est.) Germany 1
Poland 1
N.Korea 2
Israel 2
France 2
UK 2
India 2

MAIN BATTLE TANKS

rest of the world 32
China 5
USA 11
USSR 34

Poland 2
Turkey 2
Israel 2
Syria 3
Czechoslovakia 3
(est.) Germany 3
Iraq 3

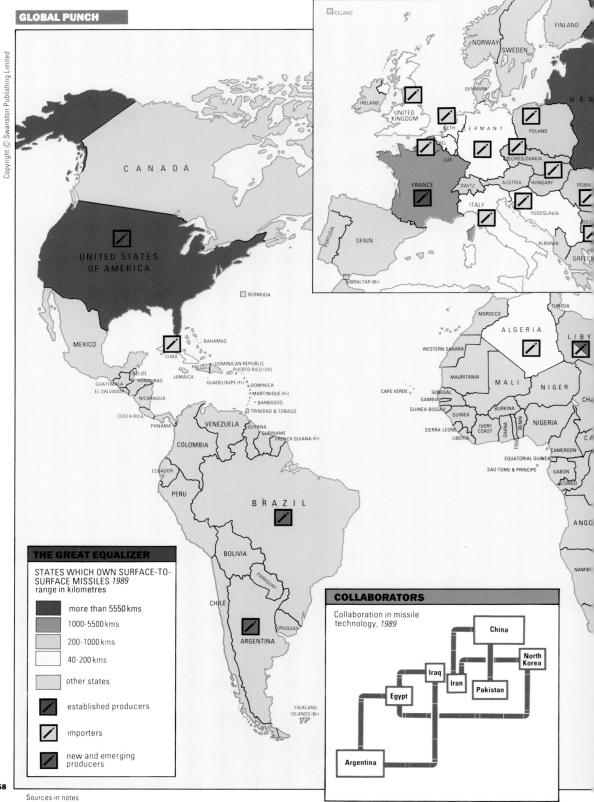

Copyright © Swanston Publishing Limited

ICELAND

FINLAND

NORWAY SWEDEN

DENMARK

IRELAND

UNITED
KINGDOM

NETH GERMANY POLAND

BEL

LUX CZECHOSLOVAKIA

FRANCE SWITZ AUSTRIA HUNGARY ROMA

ITALY YUGOSLAVIA BULG

PORTUGAL ALBANIA

SPAIN GREECE

U S S

CANADA

BERMUDA

UNITED STATES
OF AMERICA

MEXICO

BAHAMAS

CUBA

BELIZE DOMINICAN REPUBLIC
HAITI PUERTO RICO (US)
GUATEMALA JAMAICA GUADELOUPE (Fr)
HONDURAS DOMINICA
EL SALVADOR MARTINIQUE (Fr)
NICARAGUA BARBADOS
TRINIDAD & TOBAGO
COSTA RICA
PANAMA VENEZUELA GUYANA
SURINAME
COLOMBIA FRENCH GUIANA (Fr)

ECUADOR

PERU

BRAZIL

BOLIVIA

PARAGUAY

CHILE

URUGUAY

ARGENTINA

FALKLAND
ISLANDS (Br)

MOROCCO TUNISIA

ALGERIA LIBY

WESTERN SAHARA

MAURITANIA MALI NIGER

CAPE VERDE CH
SENEGAL
GAMBIA
GUINEA-BISSAU BURKINA NIGERIA
GUINEA
SIERRA LEONE IVORY GHANA BENIN
COAST TOGO CA
LIBERIA
CAMEROON
EQUATORIAL GUINEA
SAO TOME & PRINCIPE GABON
CONGO

ANGO

NAMIBI

THE GREAT EQUALIZER

STATES WHICH OWN SURFACE-TO-
SURFACE MISSILES *1989*
range in kilometres

more than 5550 kms

1000-5500 kms

200-1000 kms

40-200 kms

other states

established producers

importers

new and emerging
producers

COLLABORATORS

Collaboration in missile
technology, *1989*

China

North
Korea

Iraq

Iran

Egypt Pakistan

Argentina

Sources in notes

Missiles permit states to launch long-range strikes on the armies and cities of their enemies. Thirty-nine states have missiles or are getting them.

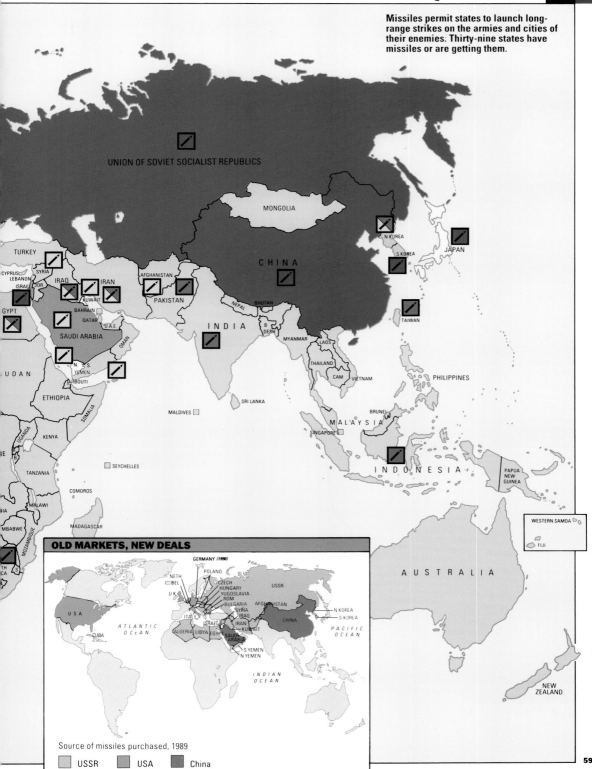

UNION OF SOVIET SOCIALIST REPUBLICS

MONGOLIA

N KOREA

JAPAN

S KOREA

CHINA

TURKEY

CYPRUS
LEBANON
SYRIA
ISRAEL JOR
IRAQ
KUWAIT
IRAN
AFGHANISTAN
PAKISTAN
TAIWAN

EGYPT

BAHRAIN
QATAR
U.A.E.
SAUDI ARABIA
OMAN

NEPAL BHUTAN

INDIA

B DESH

MYANMAR

LAOS

THAILAND

CAM VIETNAM

PHILIPPINES

UDAN

N. S.
YEMEN
DJIBOUTI

ETHIOPIA

SOMALIA

UGANDA

KENYA

SRI LANKA

MALDIVES

BRUNEI

MALAYSIA

SINGAPORE

TANZANIA

COMOROS

SEYCHELLES

INDONESIA

PAPUA
NEW
GUINEA

MALAWI

MADAGASCAR

MBABWE

MOZAMBIQUE

AUSTRALIA

WESTERN SAMOA

FIJI

OLD MARKETS, NEW DEALS

GERMANY (1990)

NETH
BEL
UK

POLAND

CZECH
HUNGARY
YUGOSLAVIA
ROM
BULGARIA
SYRIA
ITALY
ISRAEL
IRAQ
IRAN
ALGERIA LIBYA EGYPT KUWAIT

USSR

AFGHANISTAN

N KOREA

S KOREA

CHINA

USA

ATLANTIC
OCEAN

CUBA

SAUDI
ARABIA

S YEMEN
N YEMEN

PACIFIC
OCEAN

INDIAN
OCEAN

NEW
ZEALAND

Source of missiles purchased, 1989

USSR   USA   China

Copyright © Swanston Publishing Limited

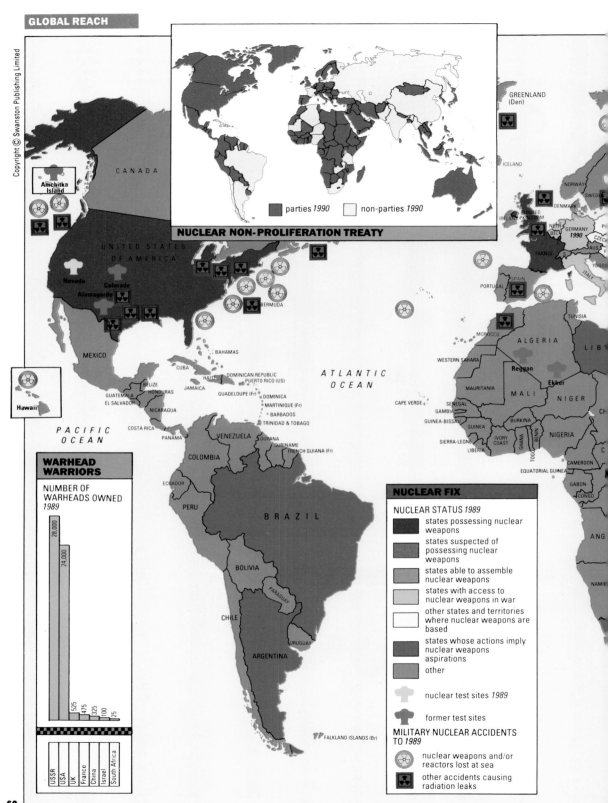

NUCLEAR NON-PROLIFERATION TREATY

parties *1990*   non-parties *1990*

CANADA

Amchitka
Island

U N I T E D   S T A T E S
O F   A M E R I C A

Nevada
Alamagordo   Colorado

MEXICO

BAHAMAS

CUBA

GUATEMALA
EL SALVADOR   HONDURAS   JAMAICA
BELIZE
HAITI   DOMINICAN REPUBLIC
PUERTO RICO (US)
GUADELOUPE (Fr)   DOMINICA
MARTINIQUE (Fr)
BARBADOS
TRINIDAD & TOBAGO

NICARAGUA

COSTA RICA   PANAMA

Hawaii

P A C I F I C
O C E A N

BERMUDA

A T L A N T I C
O C E A N

CAPE VERDE

GREENLAND
(Den)

ICELAND

NORWAY   SWEDEN

DENMARK
UNITED KINGDOM
IRELAND
NETH
BELG   GERMANY
1990
FRANCE   CZECH
AUST
YUGO
ITALY

PORTUGAL   SPAIN

MOROCCO   TUNISIA

WESTERN SAHARA   ALGERIA   LIBY

Reggan   Ekker

MAURITANIA   MALI   NIGER   CH

SENEGAL
GAMBIA
GUINEA-BISSAU   GUINEA   BURKINA
IVORY   GHANA   BENIN   NIGERIA
SIERRA-LEONE   COAST   TOGO
LIBERIA

CAMEROON
EQUATORIAL GUINEA

GABON   CONGO

ANG

NAMIE

VENEZUELA
COLOMBIA
GUYANA
SURINAME
FRENCH GUIANA (Fr)

ECUADOR

PERU

B R A Z I L

BOLIVIA

PARAGUAY

CHILE

URUGUAY

ARGENTINA

FALKLAND ISLANDS (Br)

WARHEAD WARRIORS

NUMBER OF
WARHEADS OWNED
1989

28,000	USSR
24,000	USA
525	UK
475	France
325	China
100	Israel
25	South Africa

NUCLEAR FIX

NUCLEAR STATUS *1989*

states possessing nuclear
weapons

states suspected of
possessing nuclear
weapons

states able to assemble
nuclear weapons

states with access to
nuclear weapons in war

other states and territories
where nuclear weapons are
based

states whose actions imply
nuclear weapons
aspirations

other

nuclear test sites *1989*

former test sites

MILITARY NUCLEAR ACCIDENTS
TO *1989*

nuclear weapons and/or
reactors lost at sea

other accidents causing
radiation leaks

There are five declared nuclear weapon states, a sixth which
has nuclear weapons but has not acknowledged it, a seventh
which probably has nuclear weapons and two more states
which can assemble them very quickly. Over 50 nuclear
weapons and 7 military nuclear reactors have been lost at sea.

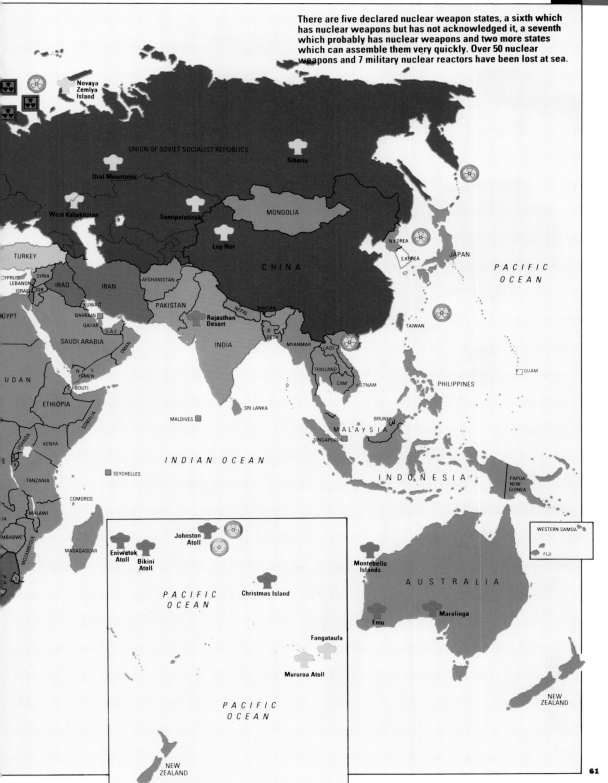

Novaya
Zemlya
Island

UNION OF SOVIET SOCIALIST REPUBLICS

Siberia

Ural Mountains

West Kazakhstan

Semipalatinsk

MONGOLIA

Lop Nor

N.KOREA

S.KOREA

JAPAN

PACIFIC
OCEAN

CHINA

TURKEY

CYPRUS
LEBANON
ISRAEL JOR
SYRIA
IRAQ
IRAN
AFGHANISTAN

EGYPT
KUWAIT
BAHRAIN
QATAR
U.A.E.
SAUDI ARABIA
OMAN

PAKISTAN

NEPAL
BHUTAN

Rajasthan
Desert

B
DESH

INDIA

MYANMAR

TAIWAN

LAOS

THAILAND

UDAN

N
YEMEN
S

DJIBOUTI

ETHIOPIA

SOMALIA

UGANDA

KENYA

E

B

TANZANIA

COMOROS

MALAWI

MADAGASCAR

MBABWE

MOZAMBIQUE

HA
S

MALDIVES

SRI LANKA

CAM
VIETNAM

PHILIPPINES

BRUNEI

MALAYSIA

SINGAPORE

GUAM

INDONESIA

PAPUA
NEW
GUINEA

SEYCHELLES

INDIAN OCEAN

Johnston
Atoll

Eniwetok
Atoll

Bikini
Atoll

PACIFIC
OCEAN

Christmas Island

Fangataufa

Mururoa Atoll

PACIFIC
OCEAN

NEW
ZEALAND

Montebello
Islands

AUSTRALIA

Emu

Maralinga

WESTERN SAMOA

FIJI

NEW
ZEALAND

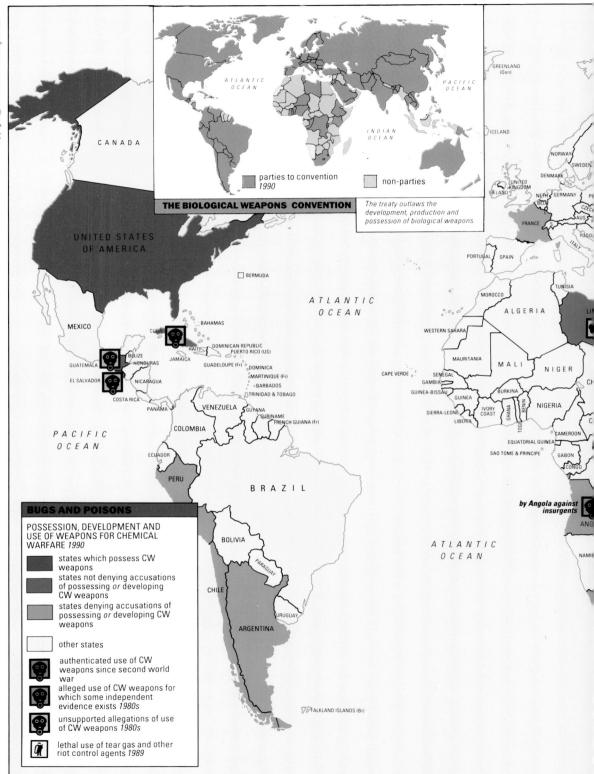

THE BIOLOGICAL WEAPONS CONVENTION

parties to convention 1990

non-parties

The treaty outlaws the development, production and possession of biological weapons.

BUGS AND POISONS

POSSESSION, DEVELOPMENT AND USE OF WEAPONS FOR CHEMICAL WARFARE *1990*

states which possess CW weapons

states not denying accusations of possessing *or* developing CW weapons

states denying accusations of possessing *or* developing CW weapons

other states

authenticated use of CW weapons since second world war

alleged use of CW weapons for which some independent evidence exists *1980s*

unsupported allegations of use of CW weapons *1980s*

lethal use of tear gas and other riot control agents *1989*

by Angola against insurgents

Sources in notes

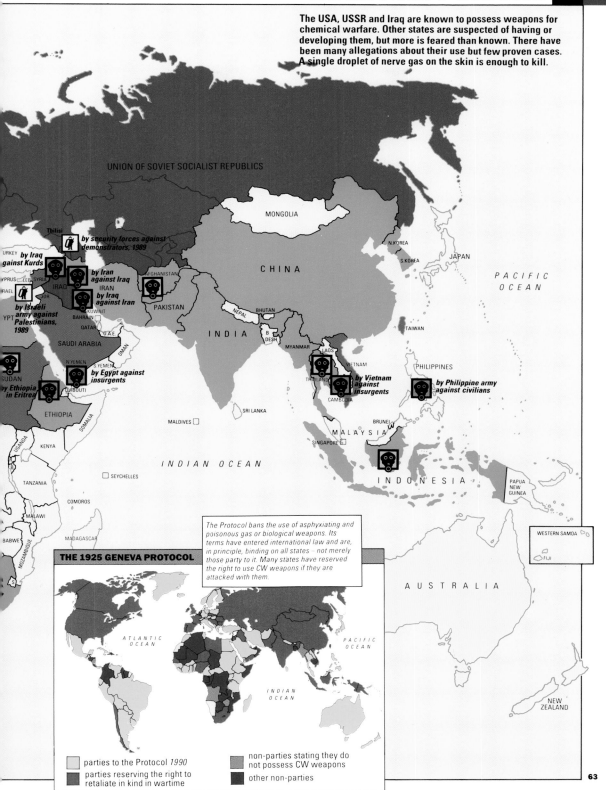

The USA, USSR and Iraq are known to possess weapons for chemical warfare. Other states are suspected of having or developing them, but more is feared than known. There have been many allegations about their use but few proven cases. A single droplet of nerve gas on the skin is enough to kill.

UNION OF SOVIET SOCIALIST REPUBLICS

MONGOLIA

CHINA

N. KOREA

S. KOREA

JAPAN

PACIFIC OCEAN

Tbilisi

by security forces against demonstrators, 1989

URKEY

by Iraq against Kurds

YPRUS LEB. SYRIA

RAEL

JOR

by Israeli army against Palestinians, 1989

YPT

IRAQ

by Iran against Iraq

IRAN

by Iraq against Iran

AFGHANISTAN

PAKISTAN

KUWAIT

BAHRAIN

QATAR

U.A.E.

OMAN

SAUDI ARABIA

N. YEMEN

S. YEMEN

DJIBOUTI

by Egypt against insurgents

SUDAN

by Ethiopia in Eritrea

ETHIOPIA

SOMALIA

UGANDA

KENYA

TANZANIA

MALAWI

MADAGASCAR

COMOROS

SEYCHELLES

MALDIVES

SRI LANKA

INDIA

NEPAL

BHUTAN

B DESH

MYANMAR

LAOS

THAILAND

VIETNAM

CAMBODIA

by Vietnam against insurgents

PHILIPPINES

TAIWAN

by Philippine army against civilians

BRUNEI

MALAYSIA

SINGAPORE

INDONESIA

PAPUA NEW GUINEA

INDIAN OCEAN

AUSTRALIA

WESTERN SAMOA

FIJI

NEW ZEALAND

BABWE

MOZAMBIQUE

The Protocol bans the use of asphyxiating and poisonous gas or biological weapons. Its terms have entered international law and are, in principle, binding on all states – not merely those party to it. Many states have reserved the right to use CW weapons if they are attacked with them.

THE 1925 GENEVA PROTOCOL

ATLANTIC OCEAN

PACIFIC OCEAN

INDIAN OCEAN

☐ parties to the Protocol *1990*

☐ parties reserving the right to retaliate in kind in wartime

☐ non-parties stating they do not possess CW weapons

☐ other non-parties

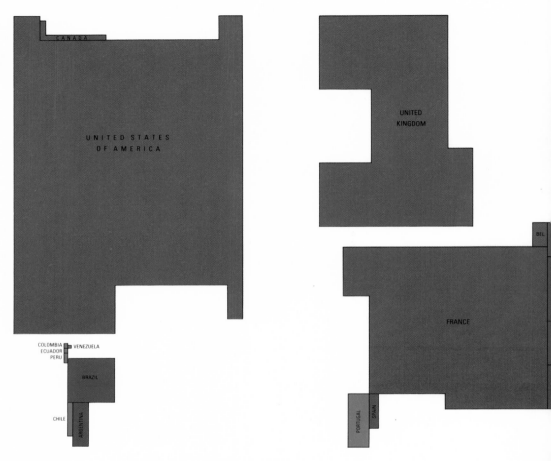

CANADA

UNITED STATES
OF AMERICA

UNITED
KINGDOM

BEL

FRANCE

COLOMBIA VENEZUELA
ECUADOR
PERU

BRAZIL

CHILE ARGENTINA

PORTUGAL SPAIN

TOYS FOR THE BOYS

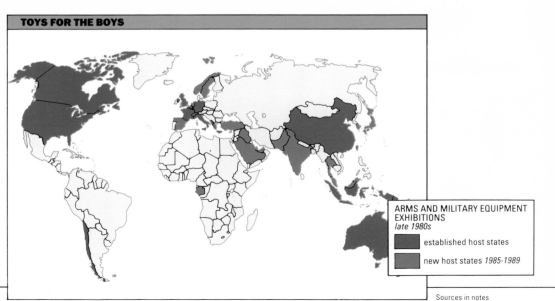

ARMS AND MILITARY EQUIPMENT
EXHIBITIONS
late 1980s

established host states

new host states *1985-1989*

64

Sources in notes

Only a handful of states can take a major weapons project from conception through development and production to deployment. They are the arms powers.

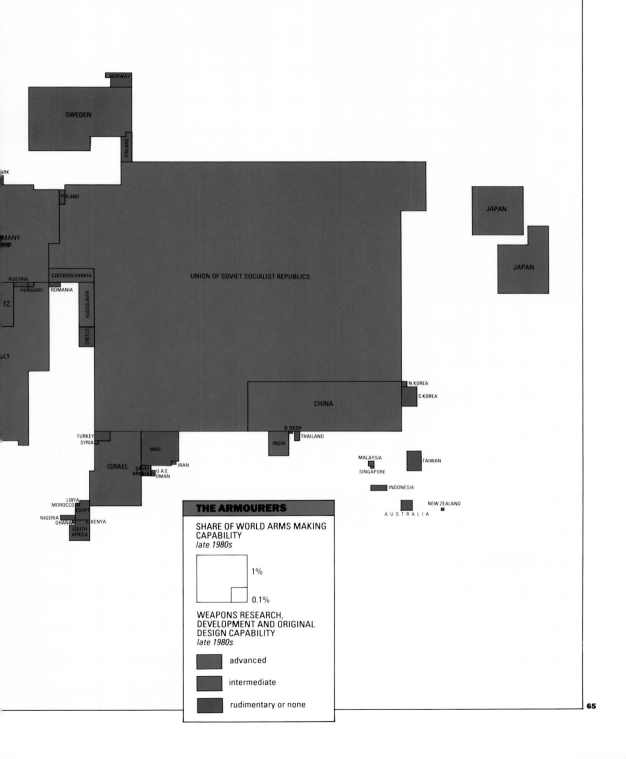

NORWAY

SWEDEN

FINLAND

ARK

POLAND

MANY
1990

AUSTRIA
HUNGARY
CZECHOSLOVAKIA
ROMANIA
YUGOSLAVIA

TZ.

GREECE

LY

UNION OF SOVIET SOCIALIST REPUBLICS

JAPAN

JAPAN

N.KOREA
S.KOREA

CHINA

TURKEY
SYRIA
IRAQ
B.DESH
THAILAND
INDIA
IRAN

ISRAEL
SAUDI
ARABIA
U.A.E.
OMAN

MALAYSIA
SINGAPORE

TAIWAN

INDONESIA

LIBYA
MOROCCO
EGYPT
NIGERIA
GHANA
KENYA
SOUTH
AFRICA

NEW ZEALAND
AUSTRALIA

THE ARMOURERS

SHARE OF WORLD ARMS MAKING CAPABILITY
late 1980s

1%

0.1%

WEAPONS RESEARCH, DEVELOPMENT AND ORIGINAL DESIGN CAPABILITY
late 1980s

advanced

intermediate

rudimentary or none

65

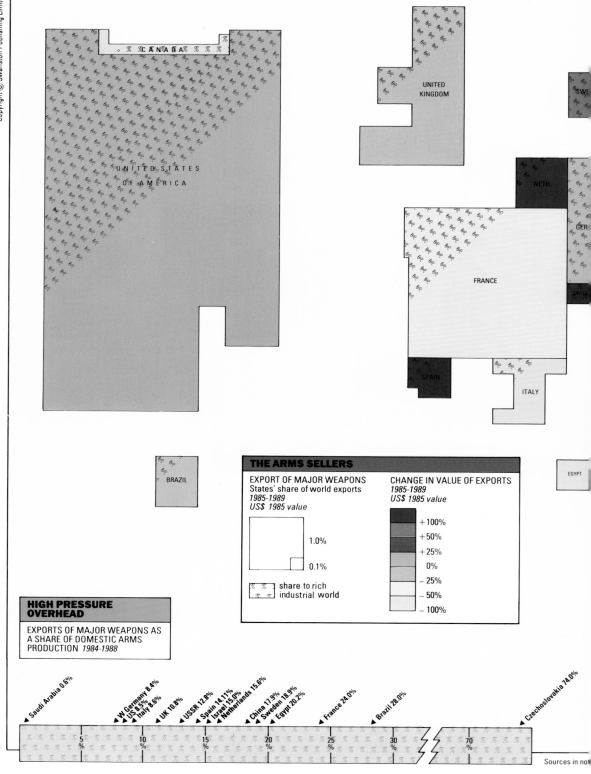

CANADA

UNITED KINGDOM

SWE

UNITED STATES
OF AMERICA

NETH.

GER

FRANCE

SWIT2

SPAIN

ITALY

BRAZIL

EGYPT

THE ARMS SELLERS

EXPORT OF MAJOR WEAPONS
States' share of world exports
1985-1989
US$ 1985 value

1.0%

0.1%

share to rich
industrial world

CHANGE IN VALUE OF EXPORTS
1985-1989
US$ 1985 value

+100%
+50%
+25%
0%
−25%
−50%
−100%

HIGH PRESSURE OVERHEAD

EXPORTS OF MAJOR WEAPONS AS
A SHARE OF DOMESTIC ARMS
PRODUCTION *1984-1988*

▲ Saudi Arabia 0.6%
▲ W Germany 8.4%
▲ US 8.5%
▲ Italy 8.6%
▲ UK 10.8%
▲ USSR 12.8%
▲ Spain 14.11%
▲ Israel 15.0%
▲ Netherlands 15.6%
▲ China 17.9%
▲ Sweden 18.9%
▲ Egypt 20.2%
▲ France 24.0%
▲ Brazil 28.0%
▲ Czechoslovakia 74.0%

5%
10%
15%
20%
25%
30%
70%

Sources in not

Not much is reliably known about arms sales, and less about their sale abroad, except that they obey economic laws more strictly than export regulations. The bigger the market, the lower the cost and the more profitable for both state and private sector producers.

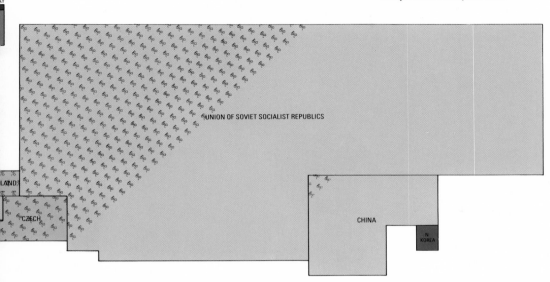

UNION OF SOVIET SOCIALIST REPUBLICS

CHINA

N KOREA

CZECH

LAND

ISRAEL

REST OF WORLD

THE REAPERS

TOP ARMS EXPORTERS AND THEIR
MAIN CLIENTS *1985-1989*
US$ 1985 value

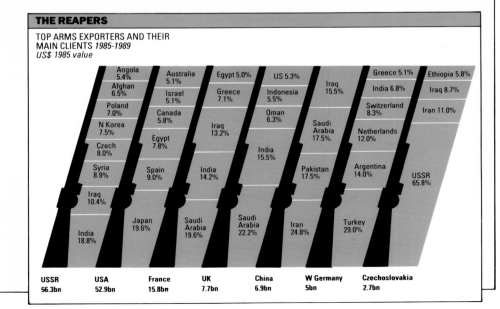

USSR	USA	France	UK	China	W Germany	Czechoslovakia
56.3bn	52.9bn	15.8bn	7.7bn	6.9bn	5bn	2.7bn

USSR:
- Angola 5.4%
- Afghan 6.5%
- Poland 7.0%
- N Korea 7.5%
- Czech 8.0%
- Syria 8.9%
- Iraq 10.4%
- India 18.8%

USA:
- Australia 5.1%
- Israel 5.1%
- Canada 5.8%
- Egypt 7.8%
- Spain 9.0%
- Japan 19.6%

France:
- Egypt 5.0%
- Greece 7.1%
- Iraq 13.2%
- India 14.2%
- Saudi Arabia 19.6%

UK:
- US 5.3%
- Indonesia 5.5%
- Oman 6.3%
- India 15.5%
- Saudi Arabia 22.2%

China:
- Iraq 15.5%
- Saudi Arabia 17.5%
- Pakistan 17.5%
- Iran 24.8%

W Germany:
- Greece 5.1%
- India 6.8%
- Switzerland 8.3%
- Netherlands 12.0%
- Argentina 14.0%
- Turkey 29.0%

Czechoslovakia:
- Ethiopia 5.8%
- Iraq 8.7%
- Iran 11.0%
- USSR 65.8%

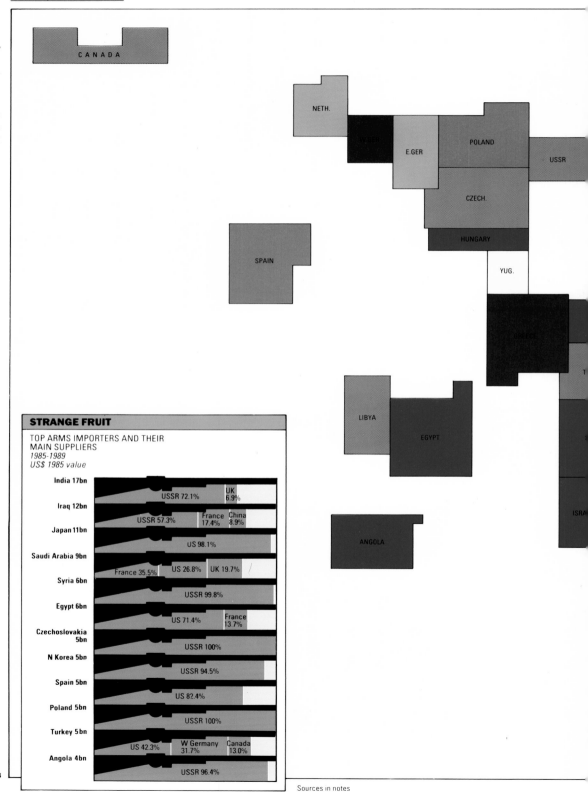

CANADA

NETH.

W.GER.

E.GER

POLAND

USSR

CZECH.

SPAIN

HUNGARY

YUG.

GREECE

T

LIBYA

EGYPT

ISRA

ANGOLA

STRANGE FRUIT

TOP ARMS IMPORTERS AND THEIR
MAIN SUPPLIERS
1985-1989
US$ 1985 value

Importer			
India 17bn	USSR 72.1%	UK 6.9%	
Iraq 12bn	USSR 57.3%	France 17.4%	China 8.9%
Japan 11bn	US 98.1%		
Saudi Arabia 9bn	France 35.5%	US 26.8%	UK 19.7%
Syria 6bn	USSR 99.8%		
Egypt 6bn	US 71.4%	France 13.7%	
Czechoslovakia 5bn	USSR 100%		
N Korea 5bn	USSR 94.5%		
Spain 5bn	US 82.4%		
Poland 5bn	USSR 100%		
Turkey 5bn	US 42.3%	W Germany 31.7%	Canada 13.0%
Angola 4bn	USSR 96.4%		

Sources in notes

A dozen states account for nine-tenths of all major weapons imports. Seven-tenths of their imports still come from just two suppliers – the USSR and the USA.

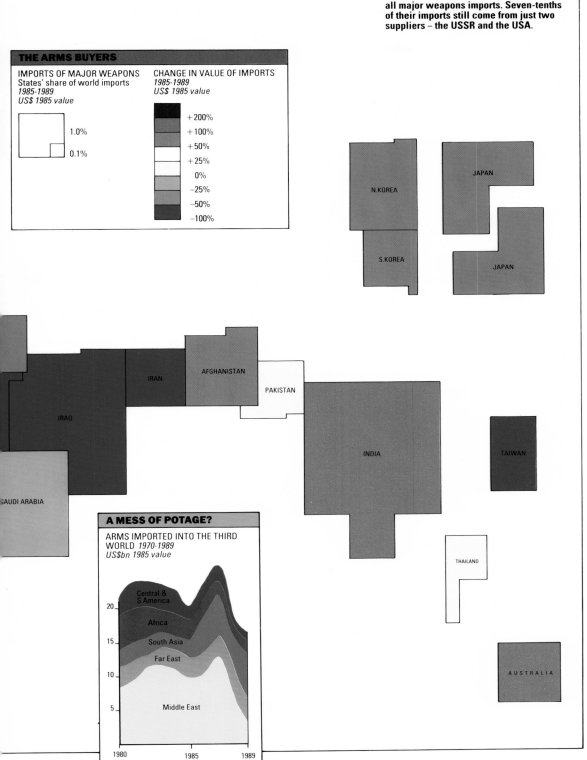

THE ARMS BUYERS

IMPORTS OF MAJOR WEAPONS
States' share of world imports
1985-1989
US$ 1985 value

1.0%
0.1%

CHANGE IN VALUE OF IMPORTS
1985-1989
US$ 1985 value

+200%
+100%
+50%
+25%
0%
−25%
−50%
−100%

N.KOREA

S.KOREA

JAPAN

JAPAN

IRAN

AFGHANISTAN

PAKISTAN

IRAQ

INDIA

TAIWAN

SAUDI ARABIA

THAILAND

AUSTRALIA

A MESS OF POTAGE?

ARMS IMPORTED INTO THE THIRD WORLD *1970-1989*
US$bn 1985 value

Central & S America

Africa

South Asia

Far East

Middle East

20
15
10
5

1980   1985   1989

Copyright © Swanston Publishing Limited

Components for
'super-gun',
seized April 1990

Machinery for testi
reliability of nuclea
warheads
South Africa

ICELAND

NORWAY   SWEDEN   FINLAND

Libya   Libya

Components for
nuclear triggers
seized by
British
Customs
officials,
March 1990

Libya
Iran   Middlesbrough

DENMARK

Iraq

IRELAND

Iran
Iraq UNITED
      KINGDOM

Iraq

Libya
Iran
Iraq
GERMANY
WEST

Iraq   Libya

Nicaraguan Contras
Afghan
Mujaheddin

POLAND

Libya   Ira
         Ar
         Ira

London

NETH

GERMANY
EAST   CZECH

Afghan Mujaheddin
Nicaraguan Contras

US

Iraq

BEL

Libya   Iraq

Afghan Mujaheddin
Nicaraguan Contras

FRANCE

Lugano
SWITZ

AUSTRIA   HUNGARY

Egypt
Libya
Iraq
Argentina

ROMA

Iraq

MONACO

ITALY

Libya

YUGOSLAVIA   BU

Barcelona

SPAIN

S Africa
Argentina
Egypt

Iraq
Argentina
Egypt

Egypt
Iraq
Argentina

Libya

ALBANIA

GREE

PORTUGAL

Shells and other equipment
for nuclear-capable artillery,
1977

Components for
'super-gun', seized April

GIBRALTAR (Br)

Ira

C A N A D A

W Germ

MOROCCO   ALGERIA   LI

Austria I
Belgium
Denmark
E. German
Japan S.
Thailand
Yugoslav
W. Germ

UNITED STATES
OF AMERICA

Shells and other equipment
for nuclear-capable artillery,
1977

S Africa

CALIFORNIA

Iraq

S Africa   Libya   Iraq   Iran
           Iran
           Iraq

Nuclear materials,
computers & machinery
for testing reliability
of nuclear warheads

BERMUDA

WESTERN SAHARA

MAURITANIA   MALI   NIGER   C

MEXICO

Iraq

BAHAMAS

CUBA

CAPE VERDE

SENEGAL

NIGERIA

CAMEROON

BELIZE

GUATEMALA HOND.
EL SALVADOR

JAMAICA

E Germany
Czechoslovakia

DOMINICAN REPUBLIC
PUERTO RICO (US)

HAITI

ANTIGUA
DOMINICA

GUADELOUPE (Fr)

MARTINIQUE (Fr)

S Africa
Shells and other equipment
for nuclear-capable
artillery, 1977

GAMBIA

GUINEA-BISSAU
GUINEA

SIERRA LEONE
LIBERIA

IVORY
COAST

BURKINA

GHANA

BENIN

TOGO

NICARAGUA

COSTA RICA

PANAMA

VENEZUELA

COLOMBIA

GUYANA

SURINAME

FRENCH GUIANA (Fr)

BARBADOS

TRINIDAD & TOBAGO

A T L A N T I C
O C E A N

EQUATORIAL GUINEA

SAO TOME & PRINCIPE

GABON

CONGO

ECUADOR

PERU

Iran

B R A Z I L

P A C I F I C
O C E A N

BOLIVIA

NAMI

ANG

CHILE

PARAGUAY

Italy
W Germany

URUGUAY

ARGENTINA

*Most suppliers in the deals shown
on this map are private companies.
In some cases they were clearly
unaware – and in others there was
no evidence that they were aware –
of the end-use for which their
products were intended; these are
the sub-contractors who supply
equipment which could have a civil
use but was actually bought for
military purposes. In other cases,
however, the companies and
governments involved knew
precisely what the deal was for but
preferred to keep it secret.*

FALKLAND ISLANDS (Br)

PSST!

THE CLANDESTINE ARMS TRADE *1985-1989*
origins and destinations as shown

Nuclear weapons programmes

purchaser   supplier   staging post

intercepted   front company

Chemical warfare programmes

purchaser   supplier

Biological warfare programmes

purchaser   supplier

Missile development/ production programmes

purchaser   supplier   front company

intercepted

Conventional forces

purchaser   supplier   staging post

Sources in notes

'In a well-executed arms deal, someone cheats everyone. It's
an exercise in pure capitalism – and it's very nasty'.
American arms industry executive, 1987

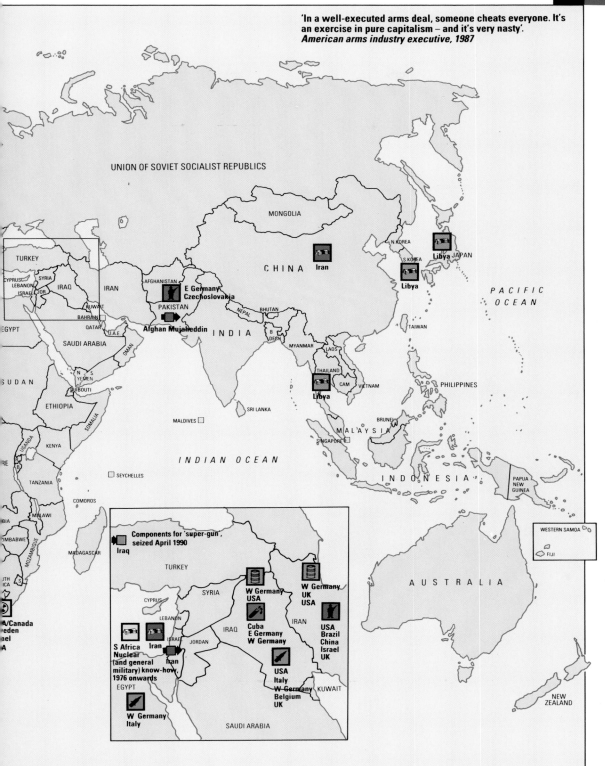

Sources in notes

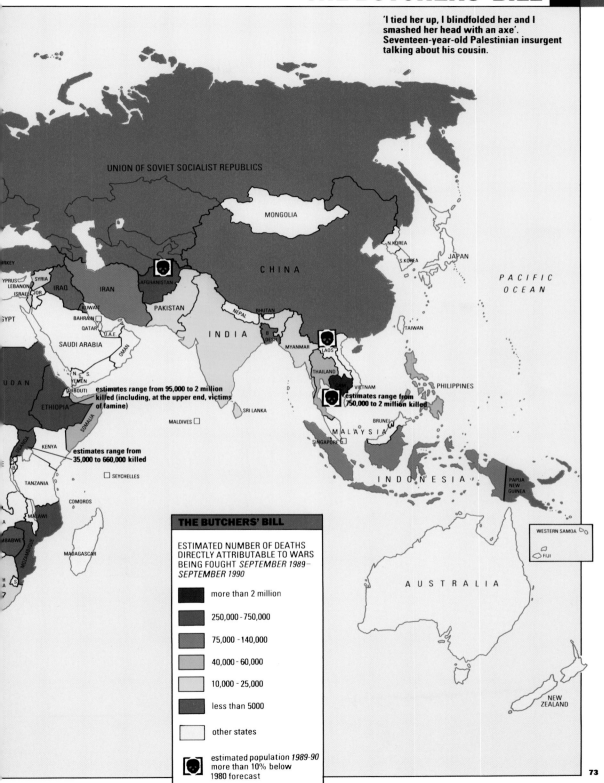

'I tied her up, I blindfolded her and I smashed her head with an axe'. Seventeen-year-old Palestinian insurgent talking about his cousin.

UNION OF SOVIET SOCIALIST REPUBLICS

MONGOLIA

CHINA

N.KOREA

S.KOREA

JAPAN

PACIFIC OCEAN

TURKEY

CYPRUS
LEBANON
SYRIA
ISRAEL
JOR
IRAQ
IRAN
AFGHANISTAN
PAKISTAN
KUWAIT
BAHRAIN
QATAR
U.A.E.
SAUDI ARABIA
OMAN
EGYPT

NEPAL
BHUTAN
INDIA
B.DESH
MYANMAR
LAOS
THAILAND
VIETNAM
TAIWAN

N. S. YEMEN
DJIBOUTI

estimates range from 95,000 to 2 million killed (including, at the upper end, victims of famine)

ETHIOPIA
SOMALIA

SUDAN

SRI LANKA

MALDIVES

PHILIPPINES

CAMB
estimates range from 750,000 to 2 million killed

KENYA

estimates range from 35,000 to 660,000 killed

SEYCHELLES

TANZANIA

MALAYSIA

SINGAPORE

BRUNEI

COMOROS

INDONESIA

PAPUA NEW GUINEA

MALAWI

MADAGASCAR

MOZAMBIQUE

ZIMBABWE

WESTERN SAMOA

FIJI

AUSTRALIA

THE BUTCHERS' BILL

ESTIMATED NUMBER OF DEATHS DIRECTLY ATTRIBUTABLE TO WARS BEING FOUGHT *SEPTEMBER 1989– SEPTEMBER 1990*

- more than 2 million
- 250,000 - 750,000
- 75,000 - 140,000
- 40,000 - 60,000
- 10,000 - 25,000
- less than 5000
- other states

estimated population *1989-90* more than 10% below 1980 forecast

NEW ZEALAND

POLAND

HUNGARY
ROMANIA

BULGARIA

LEBAN

HAITI

CYPRUS

CUBA

GUATEMALA

WESTERN
SAHARA

EL SALVADOR

MAURITANIA

CHAD

HONDURAS

SENEGAL

GUINEA-BISSAU

SUDAN

ETHIOPIA

NICARAGUA

SURINAME

SOMALIA

PERU

CHILE

ZAIRE

RWANDA

UGANDA

BURUNDI

ANGOLA

MOZAMBIQUE

NAMIBIA

SOUTH AFRICA

▲ Namibia 1: 43
40,000

▲ Australia 1:109
151,000

▲ Canada 1:117
224,000

▲ Sweden 1:126
87,000

▲ Denmark 1:192
27,000

▲ USA 1:211
1.2m

▲ France 1:330 **170,000**
▲ Switzerland 1:330 **20,000**
▲ New Zealand 1:357
9,000

▲ Austria 1:455
17,000

Sources in notes

At the end of the 1980s there were at least 35 million refugees in the world, driven from home by war, abuse and fear. More than half of them were fugitives in their own countries. In 1990 Iraq added about a million to their numbers.

USSR

AFGHANISTAN

IRAN

ISRAEL

CHINA

INDIA

BANGLADESH

MYANMAR

LAOS

SRI LANKA

CAMBODIA

VIETNAM

PHILIPPINES

S.YEMEN

THE DISPLACED

CONTRIBUTORS TO WORLD
REFUGEE POPULATION
end 1980s

1%

0.1%

INTERNAL REFUGEES AS A
PROPORTION OF ALL REFUGEES
CREATED BY EACH STATE
percentages

100
75
50
25
0

INDONESIA

MELTING POTS

Ratio of refugees absorbed to
population and total numbers
1975-1987

◄ W.Germany 1:855
71,000

◄ Netherlands 1:973
15,000

◄ Spain 1:276
31,000

WORLD REFUGEE POPULATION
1981-1988 millions

1981 1982 1983 1984 1985 1986 1987 1988

23 19 18 21 23 27 31 33

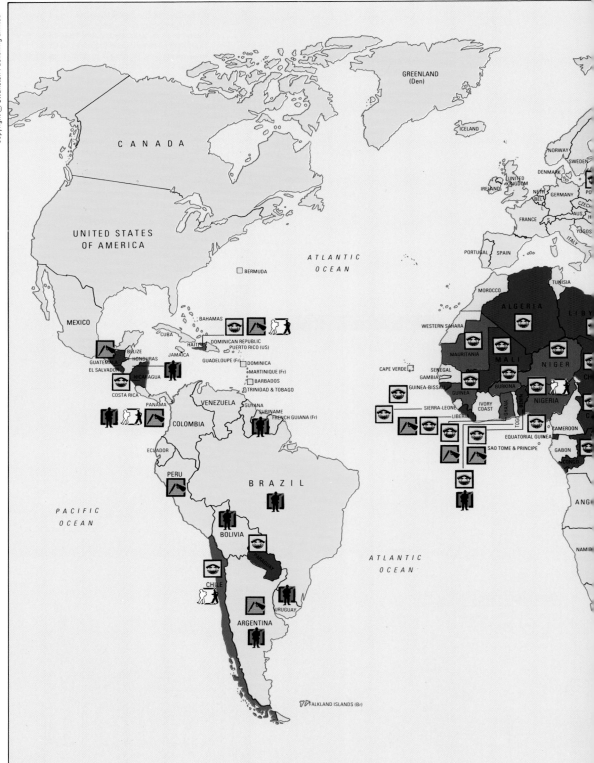

Sources in notes

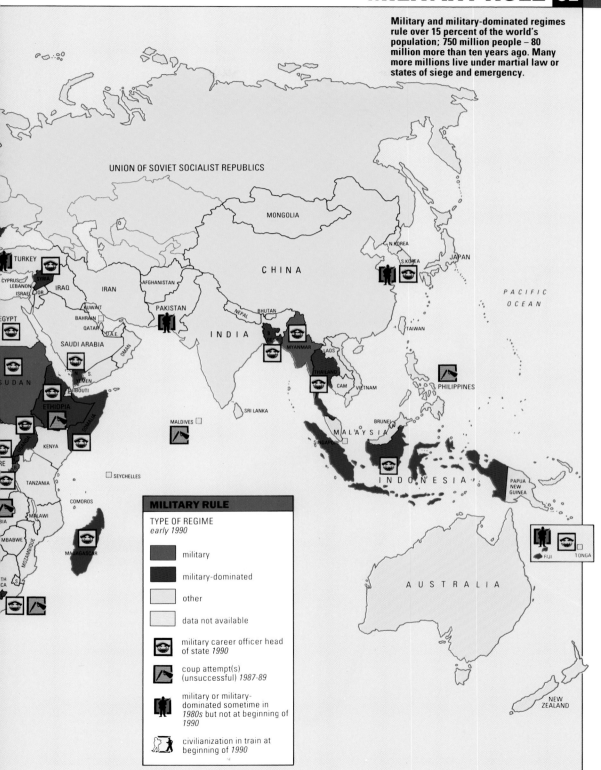

Military and military-dominated regimes rule over 15 percent of the world's population; 750 million people – 80 million more than ten years ago. Many more millions live under martial law or states of siege and emergency.

UNION OF SOVIET SOCIALIST REPUBLICS

MONGOLIA

CHINA

N KOREA

S KOREA

JAPAN

PACIFIC OCEAN

TURKEY

CYPRUS
LEBANON
ISRAEL JOR
SYRIA
IRAQ

IRAN

AFGHANISTAN

KUWAIT
BAHRAIN
QATAR
U.A.E.
OMAN

PAKISTAN

NEPAL
BHUTAN

INDIA

TAIWAN

EGYPT

SAUDI ARABIA

N.S.
YEMEN
DJIBOUTI

SUDAN

ETHIOPIA

SOMALIA

KENYA

MALDIVES

SRI LANKA

MYANMAR

LAOS

THAILAND

CAM
VIETNAM

PHILIPPINES

BRUNEI

MALAYSIA

SINGAPORE

INDONESIA

PAPUA
NEW
GUINEA

TANZANIA

COMOROS

SEYCHELLES

MALAWI

MBABWE

MOZAMBIQUE

MADAGASCAR

FIJI

TONGA

AUSTRALIA

NEW
ZEALAND

MILITARY RULE

TYPE OF REGIME
early 1990

- military
- military-dominated
- other
- data not available

military career officer head of state *1990*

coup attempt(s) (unsuccessful) *1987-89*

military or military-dominated sometime in *1980s* but not at beginning of *1990*

civilianization in train at beginning of *1990*

GREENLAND
(Den)

ICELAND

NORWAY
SWEDEN

DENMARK

IRELAND
UNITED
KINGDOM

NETH.
BEL.
GERMANY
CZECH.
AUS.

FRANCE
S.

ITALY

PORTUGAL
SPAIN

C A N A D A

TUNISIA

MOROCCO

ALGERIA
LIB

UNITED STATES
OF AMERICA

ATLANTIC
OCEAN

BERMUDA

WESTERN SAHARA

MAURITANIA
MALI
NIGER

MEXICO

BAHAMAS

CUBA
HAITI
JAMAICA
DOMINICAN REPUBLIC
PUERTO RICO (US)
GUADELOUPE (Fr)
DOMINICA
MARTINIQUE (Fr)
BARBADOS
TRINIDAD & TOBAGO

CAPE VERDE

SENEGAL
GAMBIA
GUINEA-BISSAU

GUINEA

SIERRA-LEONE

BURKINA

IVORY
COAST
GHANA

BENIN

NIGERIA

C

GUATEMALA
BELIZE
HONDURAS
EL SALVADOR
NICARAGUA
COSTA RICA
PANAMA

LIBERIA
TOGO

CAMEROON

VENEZUELA
GUYANA
SURINAME
FRENCH GUIANA (Fr)

EQUATORIAL GUINEA
SAO TOME & PRINCIPE

GABON
CONGO

COLOMBIA

ECUADOR

PERU

B R A Z I L

ANG

BOLIVIA

PACIFIC
OCEAN

PARAGUAY

CHILE

URUGUAY

ARGENTINA

NAMIB

FALKLAND ISLANDS (Br)

OFFICIAL TERROR

**STATE TERRORIST ACTIVITIES
REPORTED**
end 1980s

arbitrary arrest and/or
sentencing and/or
punishment

brutal treatment and/or
torture in custody plus the
above

assassinations and/or
disappearances plus the
above

other states

death sentences carried out
for anti-state activity or
sentiment *1985–mid-1988*

armed forces engaged in
civil war/violent policing
1985-90

Sources in notes

States' use of terror to affect the
behaviour of citizens is commonplace.
Fifty-one states employ assassination and
abduction; 115 resort to torture or brutal
treatment in detention; 125 to arbitrary
action by police and judges.

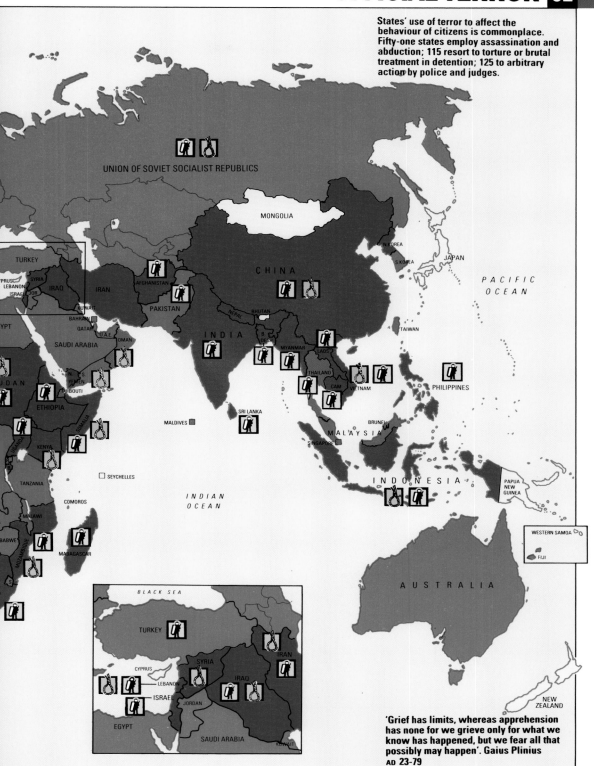

UNION OF SOVIET SOCIALIST REPUBLICS

MONGOLIA

TURKEY

CYPRUS
LEBANON
SYRIA
ISRAEL
JOR
IRAQ
IRAN
KUWAIT
BAHRAIN
QATAR
U.A.E.
OMAN
SAUDI ARABIA
EGYPT

N. YEMEN
S. YEMEN
DJIBOUTI
ETHIOPIA
SOMALIA
UGANDA
KENYA
TANZANIA
COMOROS
MALAWI
ZIMBABWE
MOZAMBIQUE
MADAGASCAR
SUDAN

AFGHANISTAN

PAKISTAN

CHINA

N. KOREA
S. KOREA
JAPAN

TAIWAN

PACIFIC
OCEAN

INDIA

NEPAL
BHUTAN
B.
DESH
MYANMAR
LAOS
THAILAND
CAM
VIETNAM

PHILIPPINES

SRI LANKA

MALDIVES

SEYCHELLES

INDIAN
OCEAN

BRUNEI

MALAYSIA

SINGAPORE

INDONESIA

PAPUA
NEW
GUINEA

WESTERN SAMOA

FIJI

AUSTRALIA

BLACK SEA

TURKEY

CYPRUS
LEBANON
ISRAEL
JORDAN
EGYPT

SYRIA

IRAN

IRAQ

SAUDI ARABIA

KUWAIT

NEW
ZEALAND

'Grief has limits, whereas apprehension
has none for we grieve only for what we
know has happened, but we fear all that
possibly may happen'. Gaius Plinius
AD 23-79

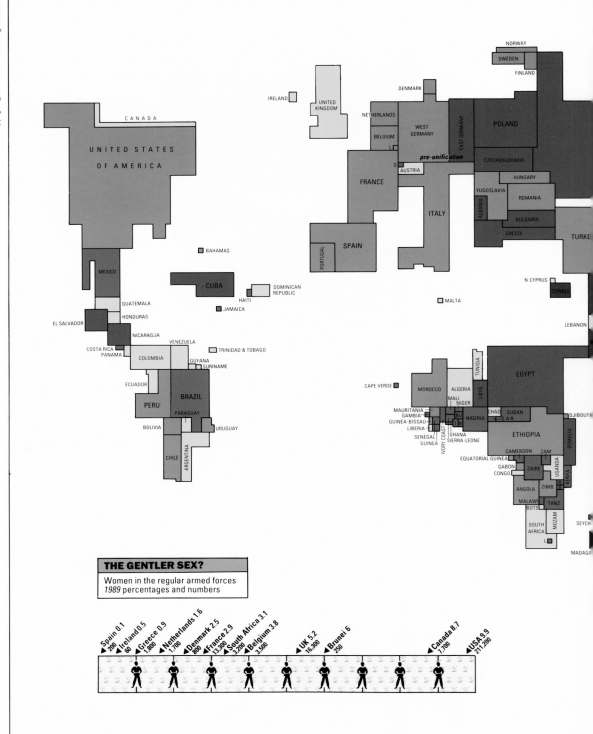

CANADA

UNITED STATES
OF AMERICA

IRELAND

UNITED
KINGDOM

NORWAY
SWEDEN
FINLAND

DENMARK

NETHERLANDS
BELGIUM
L
S
AUSTRIA

WEST
GERMANY
EAST GERMANY
pre-unification

POLAND

CZECHOSLOVAKIA

HUNGARY

FRANCE

ITALY

YUGOSLAVIA
ALBANIA

ROMANIA

BULGARIA
GREECE

TURKE

BAHAMAS

MEXICO

CUBA

DOMINICAN
REPUBLIC
HAITI

JAMAICA

GUATEMALA

HONDURAS

EL SALVADOR

NICARAGUA

COSTA RICA
PANAMA

VENEZUELA

COLOMBIA

GUYANA
SURINAME

TRINIDAD & TOBAGO

ECUADOR

PERU

BRAZIL

PARAGUAY

BOLIVIA

URUGUAY

CHILE

ARGENTINA

PORTUGAL

SPAIN

MALTA

N. CYPRUS
CYPRUS

LEBANON

CAPE VERDE

MOROCCO

ALGERIA

TUNISIA
LIBYA

EGYPT

MAURITANIA
GAMBIA
GUINEA-BISSAU
LIBERIA

SENEGAL
GUINEA

MALI
NIGER
BU
T B
IVORY COAST
GHANA
SIERRA LEONE

NIGERIA

CHAD
C A R

SUDAN

DJIBOUTI

ETHIOPIA

SOMALIA

CAMEROON
EQUATORIAL GUINEA
GABON
CONGO

ZAIRE

ZAM

UGANDA
KENYA

ANGOLA

ZIMB
MALAWI
BOTS
TANZ
MOZAM

SOUTH
AFRICA

SEYCH

L

MADAGA

Sources in notes

THE GENTLER SEX?

Women in the regular armed forces
1989 percentages and numbers

Spain 0.1 / 200
Ireland 0.5 / 60
Greece 0.9 / 1,800
Netherlands 1.6 / 1,700
Denmark 2.5 / 800
France 2.9 / 13,300
South Africa 3.1 / 3,200
Belgium 3.8 / 3,500
UK 5.2 / 16,300
Brunei 6 / 250
Canada 8.7 / 7,700
USA 9.9 / 211,200

There are over 35 million people serving full-time in the world's military and para-military forces, about one in twenty of young adult men.

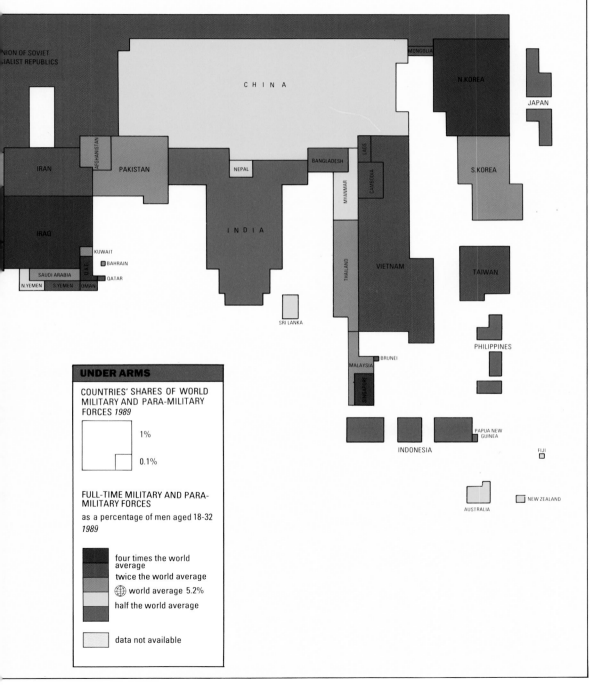

UNDER ARMS

COUNTRIES' SHARES OF WORLD MILITARY AND PARA-MILITARY FORCES *1989*

1%

0.1%

FULL-TIME MILITARY AND PARA-MILITARY FORCES

as a percentage of men aged 18-32 *1989*

four times the world average
twice the world average
⊕ world average 5.2%
half the world average

data not available

81

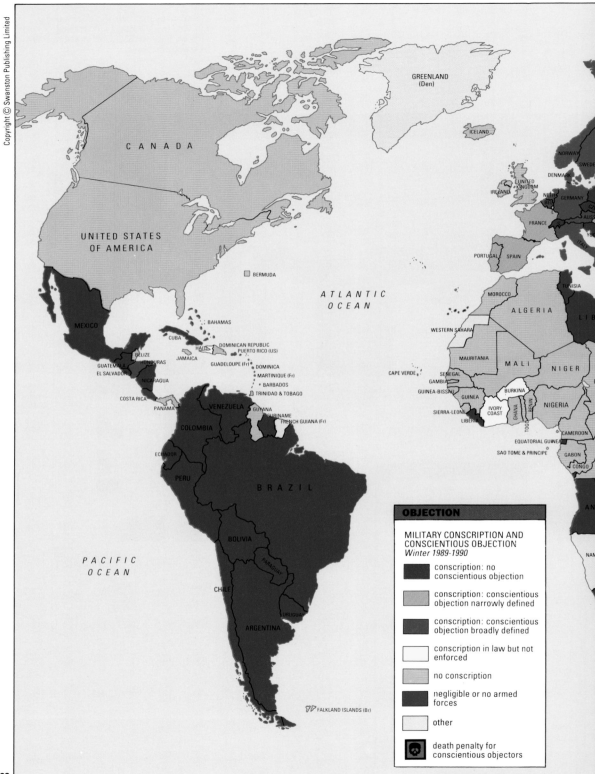

GREENLAND
(Den)

ICELAND

NORWAY
SWEDEN
DENMARK
UNITED
KINGDOM
IRELAND
NETHS GERMANY
FRANCE
AUS
ITALY
YUG

C A N A D A

UNITED STATES
OF AMERICA

BERMUDA

ATLANTIC
OCEAN

PORTUGAL SPAIN

MOROCCO

TUNISIA

ALGERIA
LIB

WESTERN SAHARA

MEXICO

BAHAMAS

CUBA
HAITI
DOMINICAN REPUBLIC
PUERTO RICO (US)
JAMAICA
GUADELOUPE (Fr)
DOMINICA
MARTINIQUE (Fr)
BARBADOS
TRINIDAD & TOBAGO

BELIZE
GUATEMALA HONDURAS
EL SALVADOR
NICARAGUA
COSTA RICA
PANAMA

MAURITANIA
M A L I
N I G E R

CAPE VERDE
SENEGAL
GAMBIA
GUINEA-BISSAU
GUINEA
SIERRA LEONE
LIBERIA
BURKINA
IVORY
COAST
GHANA
TOGO
BENIN
NIGERIA

VENEZUELA
GUYANA
SURINAME
FRENCH GUIANA (Fr)

COLOMBIA

ECUADOR

EQUATORIAL GUINEA
SAO TOME & PRINCIPE
CAMEROON
GABON
CONGO

PERU

B R A Z I L

ANG

PACIFIC
OCEAN

BOLIVIA

PARAGUAY

NAM

CHILE

URUGUAY

ARGENTINA

FALKLAND ISLANDS (Br)

OBJECTION

MILITARY CONSCRIPTION AND
CONSCIENTIOUS OBJECTION
Winter 1989-1990

- conscription: no conscientious objection
- conscription: conscientious objection narrowly defined
- conscription: conscientious objection broadly defined
- conscription in law but not enforced
- no conscription
- negligible or no armed forces
- other
- death penalty for conscientious objectors

Sources in notes

Some states with military conscription accept conscientious objection based on moral or religious grounds. Some do so grudgingly. Others do not. No state officially recognizes conscientious objection based on political conviction.

UNION OF SOVIET SOCIALIST REPUBLICS

MONGOLIA

TURKEY

CYPRUS
LEBANON
ISRAEL
JOR
SYRIA
IRAQ
IRAN
AFGHANISTAN

EGYPT

SAUDI ARABIA

KUWAIT
BAHRAIN
QATAR
U.A.E.
OMAN

PAKISTAN

NEPAL
BHUTAN

INDIA

B
DESH

MYANMAR

CHINA

N KOREA
S KOREA

JAPAN

TAIWAN

PACIFIC
OCEAN

SUDAN

N S
YEMEN
DJIBOUTI

ETHIOPIA

SOMALIA

LAOS

THAILAND

CAM
VIETNAM

PHILIPPINES

UGANDA
KENYA

MALDIVES

SRI LANKA

BRUNEI
W

MALAYSIA
SINGAPORE

TANZANIA

SEYCHELLES

INDONESIA

PAPUA
NEW
GUINEA

COMOROS

MALAWI

BIA

MADAGASCAR

ZIMBABWE
MOZAMBIQUE

NTH
CA

INDIAN
OCEAN

WESTERN SAMOA

FIJI

AUSTRALIA

NEW
ZEALAND

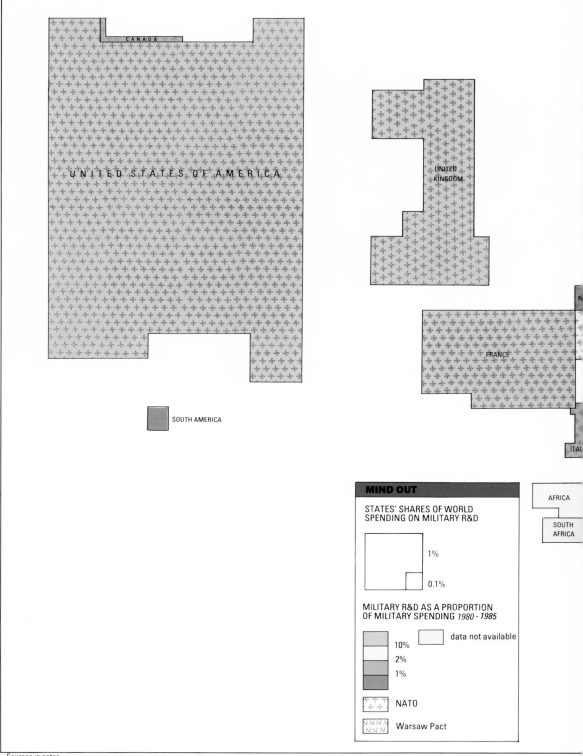

CANADA

UNITED STATES OF AMERICA

UNITED KINGDOM

FRANCE

N

ITAL

SOUTH AMERICA

AFRICA

SOUTH AFRICA

MIND OUT

STATES' SHARES OF WORLD
SPENDING ON MILITARY R&D

1%

0.1%

MILITARY R&D AS A PROPORTION
OF MILITARY SPENDING *1980 - 1985*

data not available

10%

2%

1%

NATO

Warsaw Pact

Today's military research and development is the first step towards tomorrow's military arsenal. Military R&D accounts for one quarter of all R&D spending and employs a fifth of research scientists and engineers. It is concentrated in a handful of countries.

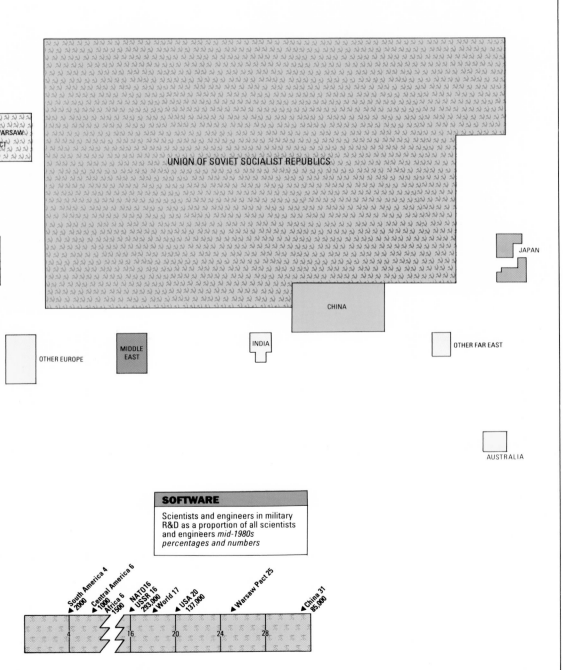

OTHER WARSAW PACT

UNION OF SOVIET SOCIALIST REPUBLICS

JAPAN

ANY

CHINA

OTHER NATO

OTHER EUROPE

MIDDLE EAST

INDIA

OTHER FAR EAST

AUSTRALIA

SOFTWARE

Scientists and engineers in military R&D as a proportion of all scientists and engineers *mid-1980s*
percentages and numbers

▲ South America 4
2000

▲ Central America 6
1000

▲ Africa 6
1500

▲ NATO 16

▲ USSR 16
293,000

▲ World 17

▲ USA 20
137,000

▲ Warsaw Pact 25

▲ China 31
85,000

4   16   20   24   28

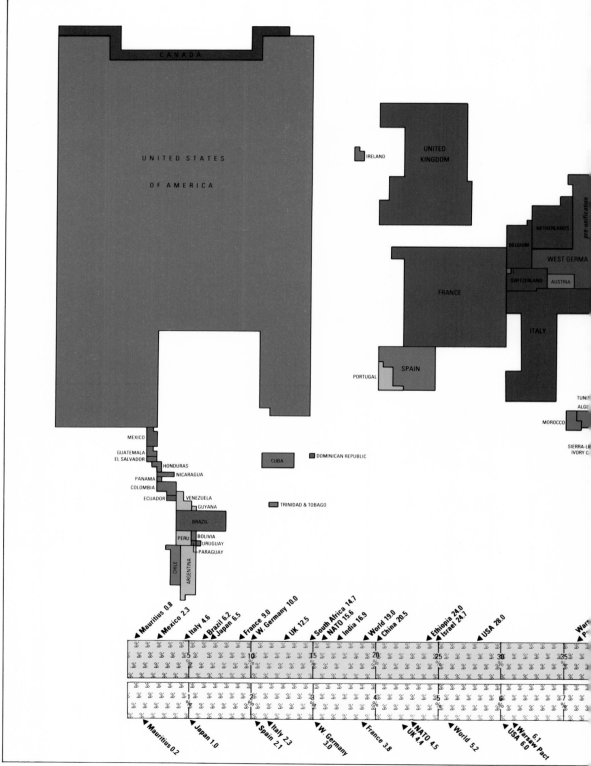

CANADA

UNITED STATES

OF AMERICA

IRELAND

UNITED KINGDOM

NETHERLANDS

BELGIUM

pre-unification

WEST GERMA

SWITZERLAND   AUSTRIA

FRANCE

ITALY

PORTUGAL   SPAIN

TUNIS
ALGE

MOROCCO

SIERRA-LI
IVORY C

MEXICO

GUATEMALA
EL SALVADOR

HONDURAS

CUBA   ◼ DOMINICAN REPUBLIC

PANAMA   NICARAGUA

COLOMBIA

ECUADOR   VENEZUELA

GUYANA   ◼ TRINIDAD & TOBAGO

BRAZIL

PERU   BOLIVIA
URUGUAY
PARAGUAY

CHILE
ARGENTINA

▲ Mauritius 0.8
▲ Mexico 2.3
▲ Italy 4.6
▲ Brazil 6.2
▲ Japan 6.5
▲ France 9.0
▲ W. Germany 10.0
▲ UK 12.5
▲ South Africa 14.7
▲ NATO 15.6
▲ India 16.9
▲ World 19.0
▲ China 20.5
▲ Ethiopia 24.0
▲ Israel 24.7
▲ USA 28.0
▲ Wars
P

5   10   15   20   25   30   35
%   %   %   %   %   %   %

1   2   3   4   5   6   7
%   %   %   %   %   %   %

▼ Mauritius 0.2
▼ Japan 1.0
▼ Spain 2.1
▼ Italy 2.3
▼ W. Germany 3.0
▼ France 3.8
▼ UK 4.4
▼ NATO 4.5
▼ World 5.2
▼ 6.1
▼ Warsaw Pact
▼ USA 6.0

The military still commandeer vast resources: **$888 billion** in 1989 – one twelfth of world output, one fifth of all government expenditure and only two per cent less than the previous year when the Cold War was still officially on.

These direct costs amounted to a thousand times the annual budget of the United Nations, or $160 for every living being. The indirect costs of military spending are incalculable.

SWEDEN
FINLAND
RK
POLAND
EAST GERMANY
CZECH
HUNGARY
ROMANIA
BULG
ALB
YUGOSLAVIA
GREECE
TURKEY
UNION OF SOVIET SOCIALIST REPUBLICS
MONGOLIA
AFGHANISTAN
CHINA
NEPAL
HONG KONG (Br)
N.KOREA
JAPAN
S.KOREA
IRAN
PAKISTAN
INDIA
MYANMAR
SYRIA
BANGLA DESH
THAILAND
LAOS
VIETNAM
CAMBODIA
TAIWAN
IRAQ
KUWAIT
SRI LANKA
BRUNEI
JORDAN
MALAYSIA
ISRAEL
BAHRAIN
U.A.E.
SINGAPORE
PHILIPPINES
YA
EGYPT
MALI
MAUR
BURKINA
SAUDI ARABIA
OMAN
INDONESIA
SUDAN
N YEMEN
S YEMEN
NIGERIA
M
ZIM
ETHIOPIA
N
CHAD
KENYA
NGOLA
TANZANIA
MOZ
SOUTH AFRICA
AUSTRALIA
NEW ZEALAND

WHAT PEACE DIVIDEND?

STATES' SHARES OF WORLD MILITARY SPENDING *1989*

1%

0.1%

MILITARY SPENDING PER HEAD
end 1980s US$

- 800
- 400
- 200
- 100
- 50
- 25

World average 160

NATO 620

Warsaw Pact 490

▲ highest: Brunei 1610

▼ lowest: Zaire 0.92

▲ Taiwan 41.5
▲ USSR 45.9
▲ Iraq 50.0
▲ Afghanistan 64.4

THE MILITARY CLAIM ON CENTRAL GOVERNMENT SPENDING *end 1980s*

40 45 50 55 60
% % % % %

percentages

8 9 10 44 45
% % % % %

percentages

▲ Israel 9.0
USSR 9.0
▲ Nicaragua 44.1

THE MILITARY CLAIM ON DOMESTIC OUTPUT *end 1980s*

ICELAND

NORWAY SWEDEN FINLAND

DENMARK

IRELAND

UNITED
KINGDOM

GERMANY

NETH

BEL

LUX

POLAND

CZECHOSLOVAKIA

AUSTRIA HUNG

ROM

FRANCE

YUGOSLAVIA

ALBANIA

GRE

PORTUGAL

SPAIN

GIBRALTAR (Br)

CANADA

UNITED STATES
OF AMERICA

BERMUDA

ATLANTIC
OCEAN

MOROCCO

TUNISIA

ALGERIA

LIB

WESTERN SAHARA

MEXICO

BAHAMAS

CUBA

HAITI

DOMINICAN REPUBLIC
PUERTO RICO (US)

JAMAICA

BELIZE

GUATEMALA

EL SALVADOR

HONDURAS

NICARAGUA

COSTA RICA

PANAMA

GUADELOUPE (Fr)

DOMINICA

MARTINIQUE (Fr)

BARBADOS

TRINIDAD & TOBAGO

VENEZUELA

GUYANA

SURINAME

FRENCH GUIANA (Fr)

COLOMBIA

ECUADOR

PERU

BOLIVIA

BRAZIL

PARAGUAY

CHILE

URUGUAY

ARGENTINA

PACIFIC
OCEAN

FALKLAND ISLANDS (Br)

MAURITANIA

MALI

NIGER

CAPE VERDE

SENEGAL

GAMBIA

GUINEA-BISSAU

GUINEA

SIERRA LEONE

LIBERIA

IVORY
COAST

GHANA

TOGO

NIGERIA

CAMEROON

EQUATORIAL GUINEA

SAO TOME & PRINCIPE

GABON

CONGO

ANG

NAM

AT THE TURN OF THE DECADE

THE CHANGING WORLD 1990

States in which major changes are:

directly related to the end of
Cold War

not directly related to the
end of Cold War

other states

THE CHANGING STATE

change in system of
government

borders changed

border or extent of territory
under pressure

conflicts which:

ended

diminished

intensified

88

Sources in notes

Much of the news was good but not all. Some of it was very bad. The end of the Cold War was affecting a lot but not everything. There were fewer armed forces but still too many. Some wars ended, but new conflicts started and many old ones worsened.

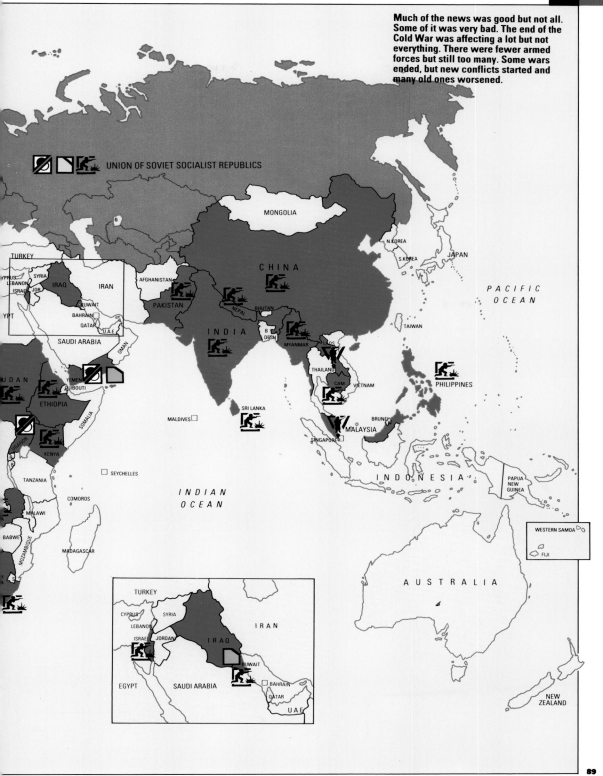

UNION OF SOVIET SOCIALIST REPUBLICS

MONGOLIA

N KOREA

S KOREA

JAPAN

CHINA

TAIWAN

PACIFIC OCEAN

TURKEY

CYPRUS
LEBANON
SYRIA
ISRAEL JOR.
IRAQ
IRAN
AFGHANISTAN
KUWAIT
BAHRAIN
QATAR
U.A.E.
SAUDI ARABIA
OMAN
YPT

PAKISTAN

NEPAL

BHUTAN

INDIA

B DESH

MYANMAR

LAOS

THAILAND

CAM

VIETNAM

BRUNEI

PHILIPPINES

UDAN

YEMEN
DJIBOUTI

ETHIOPIA

SOMALIA

MALDIVES

SRI LANKA

MALAYSIA

SINGAPORE

KENYA

UGANDA

TANZANIA

SEYCHELLES

COMOROS

INDIAN OCEAN

INDONESIA

PAPUA NEW GUINEA

MALAWI

MADAGASCAR

BABWE

MOZAMBIQUE

WESTERN SAMOA

FIJI

AUSTRALIA

NEW ZEALAND

TURKEY

CYPRUS
LEBANON
SYRIA
ISRAEL
JORDAN
IRAQ
IRAN
KUWAIT
BAHRAIN
QATAR
U.A.E.

EGYPT

SAUDI ARABIA

NOTES

1 THE DOVE OF PEACE

At the end of the 1980s, the dove of peace was seen aloft. The Cold War ended and the prospects for arms cuts improved. Several Third World conflicts also ended or eased. Yet at the start of the 1990s, the world remained a dangerous and conflict-ridden place. Had nothing changed?

On a global level, the real possibility of total war and total destruction was removed. The risk of all-out thermonuclear war between the superpowers became little more than a theoretical possibility. The ending of the Cold War liberated minds and imaginations. As foreign forces prepared to withdraw it seemed as if both war and the ritual of confrontation were on their way out. There are after all no safe havens even for the most powerful and ruthless; this was perhaps being recognized, even by the powerful, maybe even by the ruthless. It became common to talk about a worldwide outbreak of peace, for in 1988 and 1989 that seemed to be happening at a quite dizzying speed.

Renewed violence in South Africa, the inter-tribal bloodbath in Liberia and above all the Iraqi invasion of Kuwait and the American-led military response – these events of 1990 brought a different, grimmer tone to the start of the new decade. The fact that the dove of peace emerged at all is heartening: it is possible to resolve conflicts, end wars and surmount confrontation. Not all hopes have been blighted. We know that peace is possible, and that is the first step towards resolving conflicts, ending wars and surmounting confrontation.

In late 1990, the auguries for some of the continuing ceasefire negotiations are reasonably favourable. There is no reason to believe the dove of peace has disappeared for the winter. But, as ever, to take to the air is difficult and to sustain flight is even more so.

Sources for map and note:
Press reports.

2 TALKS AND TREATIES

Diplomacy is not always about cooperation and making peace; it is equally often a restrained pursuit of conflict. But the greater speed of communications means that the planet has shrunk. And this has increased the opportunities for mediating in conflicts, and for finding safe channels to negotiate them and for achieving, if not peace, at least stand-offs and ceasefires.

There is now also extensive diplomatic experience of negotiating limits and restrictions on armaments. That expertise means that technical obstacles to arms control agreements have diminished markedly over the past thirty years. Alone, diplomacy cannot achieve agreements to cut military hardware; for that, political will is required. But it creates the possibility of agreement upon which the political will can go to work.

Arms control agreements deal with limited aspects of the larger problem of armament: with particular types of weapon, from the Geneva Protocol of 1925 to the Inhumane Weapons Convention of 1981; with their deployment in particular places (the Antarctic Treaty, the Outer Space Treaty and the regional Nuclear-Free Zone Treaties of Tlatelolco and Rarotonga (see Map 13: Pax Pacifica) or with other features such as nuclear testing and proliferation.

One treaty has been excluded from the map – the Seabed Treaty of 1971. This prohibits placing weapons of mass destruction on the ocean floor. But any state with the **91** technological capacity to do this would, of course, have the capacity to make the weapons mobile and therefore more useful by putting them in submarines. Among the cognoscenti of arms control, the treaty is often likened to an agreement not to bolt aircraft to the runway. We found ourselves unable to treat it as a serious achievement.

The other eight arms control treaties which are open for all states to sign (or, in the case of the Antarctic Treaty, all members of the United Nations) have been useful prohibitions. In brief, their terms are as follows:

● The Geneva Protocol bans the use of asphyxiating and poisonous gases.
● The Antarctic Treaty bans military deployments in Antarctica.
● The Partial Test Ban Treaty prohibits nuclear testing in the atmosphere, in the sea or in outer space.
● The Outer Space Treaty bans placing weapons of mass destruction in orbit or anywhere else in outer space including on celestial bodies.
● The Non-Proliferation Treaty (see Map 23: The Nuclear Fix) outlaws the transfer of nuclear weapons technology to non-nuclear weapon states and establishes a system of safeguards against diverting materials from ostensibly civil to military nuclear applications.
● The Biological Warfare Convention bans developing, producing, acquiring or stockpiling bacteriological weapons (see Map 24).
● The Environmental Modification Convention prohibits the military use of techniques for modifying the natural environment with widespread, long-lasting or severe effects.
● The Inhumane Weapons Convention is an 'umbrella treaty' under which agreements may be reached on specific weapons. So far it bans the use of weapons that cause injury with fragments which X-rays cannot detect, and it bans or restricts the use of mines, booby-traps and incendiary weapons.

All these treaties have flaws, or loopholes. Under the Geneva Protocol, numerous states have reserved the right to use poison gas if their enemies do so first. The Partial Test Ban Treaty was indeed partial, a clean air measure, no more; the average number of nuclear tests each year increased after it was agreed. The Outer Space Treaty is vague on the definition of weapons of mass destruction and does not prevent the militarization of space. The Non-Proliferation Treaty does not ban the spread of nuclear power, the technical basis for the proliferation of nuclear weapons, and allows states to conduct 'peaceful nuclear explosions'. The Biological Warfare Convention has weak clauses on verifying compliance. The Environmental Modification Convention restricts itself by using vague terms such as 'widespread' to describe the effects of the weapons it applies to. The agreements under the Inhumane Weapons Convention restrict rather than ban some particularly gruesome weapons.

But the greatest flaw in the whole system of bans and treaties is that states choose whether or not to accept all these prohibitions and restrictions. This is also true of the regional arms control agreements. Argentina, Brazil and Chile have all defined their adherence to the Treaty of Tlatelolco which, in principle, makes Latin America a nuclear-free zone in a way that effectively exempts them from its provisions. In signing the Protocols attached to the Treaty (one seeking the support and compliance of outside states with territory in the treaty zone, the other seeking the same from the nuclear weapon states) Britain, France and the USA all attached important reservations – expressed as 'interpretations' – designed to allow them to do pretty much as they wanted. In the case of the Treaty of Rarotonga, which establishes a nuclear-free zone in the South Pacific (see Map 13: Pax Pacifica) the same three states have simply declined to sign the Protocols, though both China and the USSR and other major nuclear powers have done so.

All that said, it is a great deal better to have some states accepting some restrictions than to have none accepting any. It lays the foundations for an array of treaties which may be expanded to take in more activities and more states. Negotiations under way in 1990 are important. At the Conference on Disarmament in Geneva a treaty to ban possession of weapons for chemical warfare is a high priority. The Vienna Conference on Forces in Europe was expected to produce agreement to cut conventional forces in Europe by mid-1991. The US-Soviet Strategic Arms Reduction Talks (START) have been
discussing a cut in strategic nuclear weapons usually described as amounting to 50 per

cent. When the fine print is examined, it will probably be more like 30 to 35 per cent.

● In addition to multilateral treaties, the USA and USSR have adopted a number of bilateral treaties and agreements:
● The 'Hot-Line' agreements (1963 with subsequent up-datings) established high speed means of communication for handling crises.
● Agreements on accidental war (1971), incidents on the high seas (1972) and preventing nuclear war (1973) were all designed to minimize the risk of nuclear conflagration.
● The Anti-Ballistic Missile Treaty of 1972 restricted each side to two systems of 100 ABM launchers each (later the allowance was cut to one system each).
● The Strategic Arms Limitation Treaty (SALT) of 1972 set a maximum number of strategic missiles for each superpower; the 1979 follow-on treaty was an attempt to refine and extend the limit, but fell victim to the new Cold War which began shortly after it was signed and was never ratified.
● The Threshold Test Ban of 1974 prohibits nuclear tests with an explosive yield over 150 kilotons.
● The Peaceful Nuclear Explosions agreement of 1976 extended the threshold ban to so-called peaceful nuclear tests.
● The Intermediate Nuclear Forces Treaty (signed in 1987, ratified in 1988) eliminated US and Soviet land-based nuclear missiles with ranges between 500 and 5500 kilometres.

In recording the number of treaties to which each state is party as of 1 January 1990 and the number of parties to each treaty, we have counted only full ratification. Signature with no further action did not suffice.

To depict the growth of routine diplomacy, we have measured change in the numbers of fully staffed active embassies, or their equivalent. Only full, permanent diplomatic missions have been counted. We have not included missions to international organizations nor have we counted technical missions devoted exclusively to trade or consular matters. In the case of shared representation we assigned the mission to the state in which the ambassador has his or her main residence - a restriction which means that we are understating the degree to which bark has replaced bite in international relations. To produce a finite percentage increase for representation of new states formed between 1973 and 1989, we assigned them a single foreign mission – that of the ruling colonial power – in the base year.

Sources for map and note:
Stockholm International Peace Research Institute (SIPRI) data; Goldblat, J., *Agreements for Arms Control: A Survey*, London: Taylor & Francis, 1982; *The Europa World Yearbooks*, 1973, 1989, London: Europa Publications, 1973, 1989.

3 FORCE FOR PEACE

Multinational peacekeeping forces cannot create ceasefires and peace agreements, but they can help to ensure they are respected. Agreeing to such forces being set up, even when the underlying causes of conflict have not been removed, is a sign of good faith which can increase general confidence in the durability of peaceful intentions. It is the modern equivalent of the medieval European practice of exchanging royal hostages.

Twenty United Nations peacekeeping forces have been set up since the UN was formed. Twelve were active in 1989, of which six had been established in 1988 or 1989. This reflects both the outbreak of peacemaking at the end of the 1980s and the renewed realization of the potential value of multinational observers.

Of course, peacekeeping forces cannot impose peace. The UN Truce Supervision Organization, set up in 1948 and headquartered in Jerusalem, has been able to act as the go-between for combatants and has monitored some ceasefire agreements but it has not been able to prevent a series of conflicts from breaking out. Similarly, the UN Interim Force in Lebanon, set up after the 1978 Israeli invasion, may have helped restrict **93** warfare in southern Lebanon but was no barrier to the Israeli invasion of 1982.

UN peacekeeping forces are made up of personnel sent by member states and commanded by an officer on secondment and responsible to the UN Secretary-General. They are established only when both parties to a conflict agree; they use force only in self-defence and are equipped only with light arms. Thus, the UN forces which fought in Korea in the early 1950s, though established under the umbrella of a UN resolution, were not, by that definition, a peacekeeping force; neither were the forces which gathered in the Gulf in mid-1990 in response to the Iraqi invasion of Kuwait (Map 6: Cradle of Conflict) nor the West African forces sent to intervene in the Liberian civil war (Map 16: The Local Powers). The size of forces has varied widely: the smallest was just two (in the Dominican Republic), the largest was 19,828 - sent to the Republic of Congo (now Zaire) from 1960 to 1964.

Of the remaining peacekeeping forces depicted on the map, only one is not under UN auspices: the Multinational Force of Observers, set up in 1982 to monitor compliance with the Israeli-Egyptian peace treaty.

Another two forces, the UN Transition Assistance Group in Namibia (UNTAG) and the UN Observer Mission for the Verification of the Elections in Nicaragua, are not formally regarded as peacekeeping but since the effect of both forces was precisely to keep peace we have ignored that distinction: the role of UNTAG was to monitor compliance with the ceasefire, ensure free and fair elections and supervise the maintenance of law and order; in Nicaragua, the UN Mission had the task of ensuring the election in 1990 was conducted fairly.

Sources for map and note:

UN Information Centre, *Current United Nations Peacekeeping Operations*, London, April 1989; *The Blue Helmets: A Review of United Nations Peacekeeping*, New York: United Nations,1985; International Institute for Strategic Studies (IISS), *The Military Balance 1989-90*, London: Brassey's, 1989; press reports.

4 THE DOGS OF WAR

War thrives, and with ever greater impact (see Map 29: The Butchers' Bill and Map 30: The Displaced). Indeed there are areas where war has continued, more or less unbroken, for more than a human generation. There, though it has never ceased to be a tragedy, it has become a norm – part of the pattern of life and politics, part of the culture. Though warfare between states continues, its declining incidence may mean it is on its way out as an instrument of interstate relations. It is still with us, however, as the Middle East showed in 1990. In this map we record all wars which occurred in the period from September 1989 through September 1990 – the turn of the decade – including those (such as in Panama and Romania) which also ended during that time. Despite the spate of peacemaking that occurred between 1988 and September 1990 (see Map 1: The Dove of Peace) nobody should doubt the grip that war still has on some regions of the world.

Not all public violence is necessarily war; we define war as an open armed conflict in which regular armed forces are engaged on at least one side, in which the fighters and the fighting are organized centrally to some extent and where there is some continuity between armed clashes. This definition is a good deal broader than is used in the literature on modern war and we identify a wider range of conflicts as war than do most sources. For example the commonly used definition of war, which restricts it to armed conflicts with regular armed forces involved on both sides, is artificial. What about guerrilla war? Equally artificial are definitions which hinge on casualty rates: some scholars argue that armed conflicts are only wars if they cause more than 1,000 deaths annually; others accept a cumulative total of more than 1,000 deaths. Since statistics of war-caused death are notoriously poor (see the note to Map 29: The Butchers' Bill), it seems odd and arbitrary to make the definition of what is war turn on the scale of killing. Even if the figures were firm enough for numerical definitions to be viable, it would still be arbitrary to declare that a conflict was not war at the 999th death, but became war at the 1,000th. Our unusually wide definition of war may mean that readers are surprised at

94 some of the conflicts which are included. But we believe it is more valid and more useful than the available alternatives.

All this said, war remains hard to define. Reality is never as simple as even its most sophisticated and subtle exposition. Are death squads, often recruited from among the regular armed forces, engaged in war or in terrorism? Does sporadic bombing signify a retreat from, a step towards, a continuation of or, perhaps, an alternative to war? Our judgements have often depended not on abstract definitions but on the specifics of each case.

Beginnings and endings are even more elusive. Modern wars – especially civil wars, but also between states – tend not to have clear beginnings and endings. They splutter, kick viciously into action, subside for a while and flare up again. Wars are not declared; they rumble and explode. Some war-prone states have gone through sharply differentiated phases in a continuum of warfare. India and Pakistan are outstanding examples; Cambodia likewise; though Vietnam was at peace in 1989 and 1990, it was another example until 1988. We have tended to subsume separate wars as one, giving the earliest starting date, when one has been succeeded by another with no real break. Thus we date war in Cambodia as beginning in 1970, though it would be fair to argue that the shifting line-up of combatants means that 1978 or 1975 would be equally convincing alternatives.

It is also difficult to separate one war from another. In China, Ethiopia, India, Indonesia, Myanmar (Burma), the Philippines and South Africa, among other places, there are several civil wars going on at once in a single state. Sometimes these spill over into each other. One is often caused by another. Information sources – even in the countries themselves – may confuse different wars, combatants and causes. We have distinguished between wars wherever we were able to do so.

The definition of different types of war presents further difficulties. The broad distinction between civil and interstate war is liable to buckle in an Afghanistan or an Angola of 1987 vintage, although not of 1990 vintage, for by the latter date the foreign participants (the USSR in Afghanistan, Cuba and South Africa in Angola) had pulled out. We classified Israel's punitive strikes against Palestinians in Lebanon as civil war with foreign intervention; likewise the Tamil Tigers' campaigns against the Indian Peacekeeping Force in Sri Lanka in the late 1980s, we classified them as civil war with foreign intervention.

No two wars are alike, so subtlety has suffered in our attempt to order the astonishing range and complexity of wars. We class as civil wars those cases where the state appears to be holding apart warring civilian factions, for example in South Africa or in the Soviet Transcaucasus, on the grounds that the state was largely responsible for creating the problem in the first place. Where a state engages simultaneously in civil and interstate war, we have classified it according to the one we deem to be dominant.

We locate wars in the countries on whose soil they are fought, ignoring in this context interventionist states, such as the USA, which pursue war at a distance. Where possible, we indicate the approximate geographic focus of wars. And where they are distinguishable one from another, we indicate where there are multiple wars in a single state. Where foreign forces have withdrawn from combat in civil wars during the period covered, but left technical advisers behind, as is the case with India in Sri Lanka, we record the later form of involvement.

There is no agreed list of wars. There are many, many lists and we have added to their number.

Sources for map and note:
Keesing's Register of World Events, Harlow: Longman; *The Europa World Yearbook 1989*, London: Europa Publications, 1989; Brogan, P., *World Conflicts*, London: Bloomsbury, 1989; Degenhardt, H.W., *Revolutionary and Dissident Movements, An International Guide*, London: Longman, 1988; Starr, R.F., ed., *Yearbook on International Communist Affairs*, Stanford: Hoover Institution, 1987; Hobday, C., *Communist and Marxist Parties of the World*, Harlow: Longman, 1986; Stockholm International Peace Research Institute (SIPRI), *World Armaments & Disarmament: SIPRI Yearbook*, 1989, 1990, Oxford: Oxford University Press, 1989,1990; Sivard, R.L., *World Military & Social Expenditures 1989*, Washington DC: World Priorities Inc, 1989; Wallensteen, P., ed., *States in Armed Conflict 1988*, Uppsala University, July 1989; press reports.

5 UNOFFICIAL TERROR

Terrorism can be defined as targeting a victim or engaging in violence in order to influence the behaviour of others, often un-named or unknown. By this definition, 'law and order' must be the archetype of terror and states the supreme terrorists. Even if the definition is narrowed to extra-legal violence, states still emerge as the greatest terrorists of all.

We explore state terrorism in Map 32: Official Terror; here we examine terrorism's private sector, or part of it, for we limit ourselves to terror which has political ends and is aimed at the agents (real or supposed) of states.

We exclude terrorist incidents related to communal, racial, religious or linguistic conflict between citizens, or to spontaneous and unplanned actions of any kind. Where possible, we exclude violent factional disputes within terrorist organizations and actions carried out for personal gain (robberies, kidnappings, hi-jackings and such like) or out of personal despair, madness or delusion. We exclude hoaxes, threats and publicity stunts as well as failed or bungled actions. And we have tried to exclude 'black' terrorism – actions clandestinely undertaken by states and blamed on their opponents in an effort to discredit them.

Political terror can be conducted either on the territory of the enemy state, domestic terrorism, or abroad, international terrorism. Like war, it is an organized challenge to state policy. It implies an alternative programme. Like war, too, it is conducted in the name of principle by people who might be, but are not always, sane, stable or sincere, operating in a fog of swirling confusions, illusions, provocations, mis- and dis-information, and its aims and methods are often difficult to discern and decipher. Though similar to war, it is not the same. Regular forces are not necessarily engaged. The participants may not be centrally organized. There may be little continuity between incidents.

There is a terrorist organization in Ecuador that goes under the resplendently zany name of 'Alfaro Lives, Dammit!' It is a deadly serious organization. The name celebrates an Ecuadorian populist and peasant leader of a bygone age. It is also seriously deadly. In some ways it serves as a model for all political terrorist groups. They act, drop out of sight, dwindle, re-form, fantasize, fragment, re-form again, attract members from among selfless saints and merciless psychopaths, act again – and all in a twilight of obscurity with dashes of publicity. Some of their actions are ambiguous, some are never reported, some are reported many times over. Responsibility for some incidents is claimed by more than one group; for others, it is denied by everybody. Little is reliably known about them. Except that they live, dammit! – and seem set to continue for as long as they can find nourishment and support in a world of social injustice and personal hurt.

We learn about them from a press whose information-gathering is less than evenly spread through the world and which is often more muzzled than the terrorists themselves. At best we get a partial, distorted view heavily weighted towards the preoccupations and prejudices of the richest, western states and their most trusted regional allies.

Sources for map and note:
Vinyard Software, Database of terrorist incidents, Falls Church, Virginia.

6 CRADLE OF CONFLICT

The Middle East's long history is characterized by interminable and bitter conflicts, regularly exploding into violence and sometimes major war both within and between states. It has been punctuated by massacres and further disfigured by dictatorship, repression and torture as well as gross imbalances in the distribution of wealth.

The human rights record in the region is appalling. Freedom of expression is rare and, where it exists at all, is nearly always extremely limited. Only Israel can claim a full formal parliamentary democracy, enjoying rights it denies to Palestinians in the occupied territories. Other states either have no parliamentary democracy, or what they have is limited by restrictions on the franchise, or on the power of the elected assembly, or on both.

96 Religious fundamentalism has power in Iran, significant influence in government policy in

Israel, and a leading role in the opposition in Egypt, Jordan and Syria. The wealth provided by oil – two-thirds of the world's known, recoverable oil reserves are in the Middle East – has been more often used to buy advanced weapons and erect monuments to glorify national leaders than to meet the needs of the majority of the region's population. Water is a scarce resource: several states rely on rivers which first flow through other states' territories; at huge cost, Saudi Arabia and Libya are extracting irreplaceable fossil water from deep beneath the desert.

Before the invasion of Kuwait in August 1990, one of the most violent wars since 1945 had already been launched by Saddam Hussein of Iraq when his forces invaded Iran to secure total rather than shared control of the Shatt al-Arab waterway (the confluence of the Tigris and Euphrates, the two great rivers of ancient Mesopotamia). Indeed, the invasion of Kuwait was partially the result of Iraq's failure to win against Iran, for that war had left it with a feeble economy, massive debts and a repressed and disaffected population. It had also left a large and growing arsenal which could be used against its small and wealthy neighbour.

As the August crisis unfolded, it became clear that its resolution, whether achieved peacefully or through war, would leave the Middle East's underlying problems untouched. The pressures of further immigration into Israel and population growth in the Arab states are likely to exacerbate many existing conflicts.

The main map offers a snapshot of the region. It identifies some of the causes of current conflict and some of the issues which may generate future bloodshed. The inset map on the Gulf crisis depicts its critical first stage and the immediate transformation of a regional into a global event. Our map may illustrate the build-up to a negotiated settlement or the build-up to war. The anti-Iraq coalition is identified on the basis both of actions and of votes in the Arab League. States not in the coalition did not necessarily support Iraq's annexation of Kuwait.

Nowhere could we find a place or a way to depict a basis for hope. If there is hope for peace in the Middle East, it lies in currents forming invisibly beneath the surface of today's politics.

Sources for map and note:
World Armaments & Disarmament: SIPRI Yearbook, 1990, Oxford: Oxford University Press, 1990; Economist, 'Survey of the Arab World', 12 May 1990; Brogan, P., *World Conflicts*, London: Bloomsbury, 1989; Carus, W.S., Evidence before the House Foreign Affairs Committee, US Congress, Washington DC: 12 July 1989; Carus, W.S., 'Missiles in the Middle East: A New Threat to Stability', Policy Focus, Research Memorandum, no. 6, Washington DC: Washington Institute for Near East Policy, June 1988; Shuey, R.D. et al, *Missile Proliferation: Survey of Emerging Missile Forces*, US Congressional Research Service, 3 October 1988; press reports; see also sources for Map 23: Nuclear Fix and Map 24: Bugs and Poisons.

7 THE THORN OF AFRICA

State structures are crumbling throughout the Horn of Africa as the mini-empires, abandoned a generation ago by the European powers, disintegrate. Peoples united by language, race, culture, religion, tradition or simply by a common experience of oppression, discrimination and economic marginalization are at war with, or simply fleeing from, the brutal and arrogant minorities which exercise state power over them. The inset map on the Gulf crisis depicts its critical first stage and the immediate transformation of a regional into a total event. Our map may illustrate the build-up to a negotiated settlement, or to war.

In Ethiopia the Mengistu-led state, based on the minority Amharas, is in retreat before the Eritreans, Tigrayans, Oromos, Afars, Bejas and others. In Somalia, the Barre government, based on the Darods (or Marehans), is engaged in genocidal war with the Isaaqs in the north. In Sudan, the government – northern, Arab and Muslim – is trying to assimilate by force the medley of tribes of varying cultures and religions who live in the south.

The tide is running strongly against the existing governments. Their major foreign patrons – the USA and the USSR – have walked away. Their successors – Middle East powers – are less able to help. The region's resources are drying up in drought and scorched earth tactics. And the rebels everywhere gain confidence with each successive defeat of government forces and with each savage reprisal that follows each defeat.

Much is at stake. The states in the Horn of Africa are themselves empires in which one tribe or cluster of tribes dominates others. The end of these intra-state empires would threaten the hold of similar state structures throughout Africa. This could result in an orgy of vengeance against the upholders of regimes which are among the most brutal, corrupt and tyrranical in the world. They cannot but tremble at the prospect, against which no amount of cash in a numbered bank account abroad can adequately protect them.

Sources for map and note:
Africa Watch, Somalia: *A Government at War with its Own People*, January 1990; Africa Watch, Sudan: A Human Rights Disaster, March 1990; Clapham, C., 'The political economy of conflict in the Horn of Empire', Survival, Sept-Oct 1990; *Minority Rights Group, World Directory of Minorities*, Harlow: Longman, (1989-90); press reports.

8 THE GREATER TREK

Reforms from the late 1970s and especially since the start of the current decade have swept away many of the underpinnings of South Africa's unique system of rigid racial segregation. Within this system, the race to which you are assigned at birth determines by law where you are allowed to live, work and own property, where you study, whether you are entitled to vote and for whom. Most of the prohibitions of petty apartheid, relating to sex, travel, leisure, health care and park benches, have gone. Other parts of the system, the components of grand apartheid – statutory registration by race, segregation of rights to land ownership, to residency in urban areas, to the franchise – are bound to go with time and as pressure is exerted in and out of the country.

But their residue is destined to remain in place for decades, resting on the extreme economic and social disparities that have formed over more than a century. Whites enjoy on average ten times the personal income of blacks. State expenditure on education is 4:1 in favour of whites. For health care, whites get between four and five times as much per head. Half of all black families live in shacks and half of all whites in what would be considered mansions in most of the world. In the ownership of productive property – the commercial farmland, the mines, the factories, the modern services – whites enjoy a near-total monopoly.

How much of this complex edifice of inequality (and the apparatus of social and political control necessary to maintain it) is to be dismantled, as well as how it is to be done, and at what pace, were at the heart of the conflicts in South Africa in 1990. Although the African National Congress (ANC) and the white government had reached a peace agreement, warfare continued. There was violence between white and black as blacks strove to redress the monstrous imbalances inherited from the past. There was violence between white and white, disputing the pace and even the necessity of adjustment. And there was violence between black and black as they fought for the right to affect that adjustment and for places in the queue of its beneficiaries. Through mid-1990 it was this latter dimension of violence – the bloody clashes between the Inkatha movement, led by Chief Buthelezi, and the ANC whose best known leader is Nelson Mandela – which seemed the greatest immediate threat to peace in South Africa. But evidence is emerging of whites fomenting and participating in the clashes and it may be that ANC-Inkatha rivalry was far from the whole story.

This map differs from others in this atlas in one important respect: it focuses on the circumstances of the conflicts in South Africa, on the central institutions of apartheid, rather than on the conflicts themselves. It is part of South Africa's singularity that not just conflict but war, and not just war but brutality is endemic to the system, rather than caused by abuses of it.

South Africa has come some way from its unique and blatant form of social discrimination, to something nearer the world norm of inequality with all its obfuscations and occlusions. The central pillars of apartheid are still standing, but only just. Their final demolition might provide materials for building a different society; alternatively, it may provide brickbats for future and more intense conflict.

Sources for map and note:
Republic of South Africa, Population Census, 6 May 1970; *Official Yearbook of the Republic of South*

Africa, 15th ed., South Africa: 1989-90; Thomashausen, A.E.A.M., *The Dismantling of Apartheid: The Balance of Reforms 1978-1988*, Pretoria (1988); press reports.

9 SIVA'S TEETH

The end of British rule in India in 1947 released forces of destruction that have not yet run their course. The new rulers tried to form nation states out of a myriad societies and cultures. The process has been painful and almost unremittingly unsuccessful. Wars have stalked the region without let-up since independence. More than ten million people have been slaughtered, have died through war-created or war-worsened famines, or have been maimed or displaced. The full number is unknown.

In India there have been and still are many civil wars, fought by groups whose composition and motives vary widely. All they have in common is a rejection of the authority and legitimacy of the Delhi government in its present form; some aim at secession, some at regional autonomy, others for a redistribution of wealth between castes or classes.

Pakistan broke out of India at the moment of independence and little more than two decades later broke in two, giving painful birth to Bangladesh. In Pakistan, there have been interludes of elected, civilian government between longer periods of military rule, but few times where civil peace has predominated over civil war. There have been three wars between India and Pakistan, two of them over Kashmir about and in which conflict rumbled in 1990.

Bangladesh itself has endured civil war for almost its whole period of existence. In Sri Lanka mounting tensions between Sinhalese and Tamils finally burst into brutal civil war with, for three years from 1987 to 1990, a major Indian intervention. Afghanistan erupted in civil war as efforts to enforce 'modernization' of the country were resisted by tribal traditionalists, and then came out of the obscurity in which it had lived for so long when the USSR invaded in December 1979. Nearly a decade later, the USSR bowed to the inevitable and pulled out; the war continued.

And no end is in sight. In India (Kashmir, Punjab, Assam and Uttar Pradesh) and Pakistan (Sind), old conflicts have produced new surges of violence. There, as well as in Bangladesh and Sri Lanka, it seems that as long as the existing states persist – which is probably for as long as those states' armed forces want to continue fighting – so long will conflict continue.

Sources for map and note:
International Institute for Strategic Studies (IISS), *The Military Balance 1989-90* London: Brassey's, 1989; Sivard, R.L., *World Military & Social Expenditures 1989*, Washington, DC: World Priorities Inc, 1989; Wallensteen, P., ed., *States in Armed Conflict 1988*, Uppsala University, July 1989; Stockholm International Peace Research Institute (SIPRI), *World Armaments & Disarmament: SIPRI Yearbook 1990*, Oxford: Oxford University Press, 1990; press reports.

10 THE VALLEY OF THE SKULLS

Wars have caused the death of more than five million people in Southeast Asia since 1945. The population of the region has suffered colonial and anti-colonial wars, communist and anti-communist wars, wars of national unification, independence and secession, drug wars, secret wars, state terrorism, communal violence. For the living, the costs can be counted in the flight and enforced displacement of millions, in widespread poverty and malnutrition, and in environmental damage. Large areas of Vietnam, Laos and Cambodia will take decades to recover from defoliation, from the debris of unexploded bombs and mines and from the destruction of irrigation systems.

The outbreak of peace in the late 1980s did not quite pass the region by – but it touched it more lightly than almost anywhere else. If it seemed that the worst of the carnage might have passed, the scale of combat and misery nonetheless remained appallingly high. In 1990, only four states in the region – Brunei, Malaysia, Singapore and Taiwan – did not face armed, internal opposition groups (though all were known to be active).

99

In Myanmar (Burma), multiple civil wars raged on; government offensives against separatist groups were intensified following the crushing of a democratic uprising in September and October 1988. Between Thailand and Laos, fighting largely sputtered to an end. In Indonesia it continued, though well below the grotesque levels of violence reached in former years. In the Philippines, after a brief period of hope following the end of the Marcos dictatorship, the wars continued. The Communist New People's Army remained a major fighting force; periodic ceasefires punctuated the war between the government and the various Moro factions but no real resolution to that conflict was found. An attempted army coup in late 1989 brought the Aquino government to the edge of defeat.

After 11 years of intervention and over 220,000 casualties including 55,000 dead, Vietnamese forces withdrew from Cambodia in September 1989. The war continued. The Vietnamese-backed government in Cambodia and the three insurgent forces it confronted reached a peace agreement under UN auspices in September 1990. But hope for peace must always be tentative while the Khmer Rouge maintains its army. When it was the government in the 1970s, it ruled through terror, massacre and the creation of famine. It long seemed intent on preventing a ceasefire, and probably agreed for fear of being abandoned by its Chinese sponsors.

Through the 1980s two small groups of islands – the Paracel and the Spratly groups – were bones of contention, primarily between China and Vietnam, partly because of the possibility of prospecting for oil, partly because of profound national rivalries and antagonism.

All the data on the conflicts and forces are thoroughly unreliable. According to the convenience of competing groups, statistics of suffering are either grossly inflated or equally grossly under-estimated. But what is incontestable is that Southeast Asia has long been torn by war. In large areas the authority of central government is either non-existent, sporadic or exerted only through brutality; effective authority is often exercised by groups ranging from democratic nationalists to opium warlords to more or less disorganized bandits.

Sources for map and note:
International Institute for Strategic Studies (IISS), *The Military Balance 1989-90*, London: Brassey's, 1989; Harkavy, R.E., *Bases Abroad*, Oxford: Oxford University Press, 1989; Turley, W.S., 'The Khmer war: Cambodia after Paris', Survival, Sept, Oct 1990; press reports; see also sources for Map 4: The Dogs of War, Map 29: The Butchers' Bill and Map 30: The Displaced.

11 THE SUPERPOWERS

The term 'the superpowers' was first used in the 1940s. It was premature, for the USSR was still a regional great power rather than a global superpower as the USA had already become. For four decades – the 1950s through the 1980s – it was valid. Though there were many differences between the USA and USSR, their military and strategic strengths were qualitatively different from those of any other state. In 1990 the term became, at least with reference to the USSR, politically outdated, even though the USSR's military might remains outstanding (see Map 19: Killing Power, Map 20: The Killing Fields and Map 21: Conventional Power).

Basing armed forces abroad extends a state's military reach and provides influence. As the Cold War ended in 1989, the USSR had 600,000 military personnel based in 11 foreign countries. The USA had fewer personnel – just under half a million – but they were based in more than three times as many countries. Its reach was longer, its influence more pervasive.

The USA's global basing network was essentially established in the late 1940s and early 1950s. Since then, there have been two major changes: the build-up in Southeast Asia during the 1960s followed by a humiliating departure in the first half of the 1970s; and the movement of forces to the Gulf in 1990 in response to the Iraqi invasion of Kuwait. In the latter, USA built on a process, lasting over twenty years, of steadily increasing its strategic access to the Gulf region. There have been other smaller changes – new bases here, some closures there – but they have not altered the underlying pattern.

The US basing network combines several different roles. Forces in Europe, Korea and

Japan have been the bedrock of the strategy of 'containment' of the USSR. Other bases – the Philippines, Diego Garcia, and staging posts such as the Azores – have also been important parts of 'containment'. In the Caribbean and the Pacific (see Map 13: Pax Pacifica), US bases are instrumental in maintaining regional hegemony. In the Caribbean, the USA still retains its base in Cuba, at Guantanamo, and had forces numbering more than 10,000 in Panama long before the December 1989 invasion. Further south, the USA has carried out a numerically modest but politically critical expansion of its military presence in Bolivia, Colombia and Peru (see Map 12: Crackdown). Finally, the importance of Middle East oil for the US and world economy has made access to that region critical. Though Washington acquired facilities in Bahrain in 1949, until 1990 the US military presence in the region was underpinned only by its Diego Garcia base in the Indian Ocean, obtained from Britain in the mid-1960s and built up during the 1970s. After the Iraqi seizure of Kuwait in August 1990, Saudi Arabia agreed to host US forces for the first time (see Map 6: Cradle of Conflict).

Soviet foreign basing has always been focused in Europe. Forces there both confronted the NATO alliance and garrisoned the countries of eastern Europe. The end of the Cold War is bringing about their withdrawal. Departure from some countries will be complete by mid-1991; from others it will take a little longer. Soviet military basing outside Europe has always been relatively modest: in the 1960s the USSR acquired access to bases in Cuba and, in the 1970s, to major naval bases in Vietnam and South Yemen (North and South Yemen united in May 1990); elsewhere it gained the use of facilities and made regular visits in a number of countries.

The superpowers have gained both strategic and political advantages from their foreign basing. But the special importance of some bases and facilities shapes political relations and the flow of influence can work in reverse. It is, for example, quite legitimate to speculate that the speed with which the US administration tried to reconstruct good relations with the Chinese government after the Tiananmen Square massacre in 1989 and the subsequent wave of political executions was not unconnected with its desire to retain its electronic intelligence installation in China.

Foreign basing is routinely a source of friction between host state – or, if not the state, the people – and basing state. The local impact of bases is widely felt as negative and destructive. Grounds for complaint and opposition range from the influence a base gives its possessor in national and regional politics, through the exclusive use of vast tracts of land, to the military's unavoidable environmental damage, to difficulties in relations between the base and local residents. The behaviour of young men in uniform frequently gives offence, especially on their first arrival, not least because of the prostitution and drug-problems which are so often a by-product of the presence of US bases.

At the start of the 1990s, foreign basing is under pressure. The USSR is withdrawing from most of eastern Europe and running down forces and installations further afield. The USA has also found the vast costs of its global network harder to afford, as well as harder to justify following the end of the Cold War. New justifications may be found, however, in the activities of Latin American drug barons and Middle East dictators.

This map depicts only the permanent foreign military presence of the superpowers. Military bases are defined as permanent installations where there are ground combat forces, or military aircraft, or both, or which are home ports for warships. In other countries, each superpower has its own support facilities – e.g. for repair, refuelling, replenishment of naval fleets – or has regular, routine access. We do not record in this map superpower naval visits, usually made as a diplomatic signal of friendship, or military personnel contributing to UN peacekeeping operations, or the Sinai force (see Map 3: Force for Peace).

Military advisers constitute a further form of foreign military presence. The definition of 'adviser' is notoriously flexible. Sometimes it means exactly what it says; other times, it means military personnel engaged in combat, usually in supervisory roles.

There are numerous oddities, confusions and gaps in the data. On American advisers, for example, the major sources are strangely coy. Some of the discrepancy between the numbers of states to which each superpower sends advisers may be because one of the functions performed by advisers is best described as 'after-sales service' in the arms trade. For Soviet exports, these advisers normally wear military uniform; for US exports, they are normally employees of the corporation which made the sale. The difference can also in part be explained because there are other ways to give **101** military advice and assistance than by sending advisers abroad. At one time or another, for example, every Latin American army has sent officers to the US military training centre in Panama. In the end, however, it is *a priori* incredible that the USA should send advisers to so few states when France sends them to 16 and the UK to 30 (see Map 15: The Lesser Powers).

The data are limited in other ways. In some countries, political considerations dictate that a foreign military presence be kept as quiet as possible. If public knowledge that there is a foreign presence is unavoidable, its extent can be obscured. And there are certain kinds of facilities – especially for intelligence – over which the attempt is made to drop an official blanket of secrecy. It has taken years of research – primarily at the Stockholm International Peace Research Institute (SIPRI), but also by groups in the USA and in many of the countries where it has bases – to unearth such data as are available. We have relied on that work and the judgements of the researchers involved, except that we have perhaps been more ruthless in excluding cases where the reported presence of US or Soviet forces appears to be a matter of no more than oft repeated rumour.

There remain gaps. The most notable one is in Soviet electronic intelligence installations. The data suggest that the USSR's network of such facilities abroad is smaller not only than the USA's but even than the UK's (see Map 15). That may be so, for the USSR uses ships in many functions for which the USA uses ground stations – space tracking, communications and intelligence, for example. But it is equally possible that the Soviet network only looks so small because the data are seriously incomplete.

Under the heading of intelligence we have included installations for various kinds of electronic spying: intercepting communications, reading emissions from major equipment including missiles on test flights, surveillance of the oceans and of space. We have excluded intelligence facilities housed in embassies and we have not included human spies.

The space-related installations recorded on the map are facilities which each superpower uses to control, track and monitor its own satellites and missiles. Ground stations for communications satellites are recorded under the heading of communications, under which we also include installations for communicating with nuclear submarines and strategic bombers, and facilities which are part of a chain of strategic and/or global communications. Radio relay stations and centres for tactical or local communications have been excluded.

The early warning radar category includes only those radars designed for spotting nuclear attack.

In the case of US bases, we ignore the formal status of US dependent territories outside the USA. We include every territory not part of one of the States of the Union on which, according to our data, there is a US base.

The end of the Cold War might seem to mean that two global basing networks, both primarily justified by reference to that confrontation, should now be drawn down. That appears to be happening with the Soviet network. But the USA's military build-up in the Gulf after Kuwait was invaded in August 1990 suggests that global military deployment has not yet had its day.

Sources for map and note:

Harkavy, R.E., *Bases Abroad: The Global Foreign Military Presence*, Oxford: Oxford University Press, 1989; International Institute for Strategic Studies (IISS), *The Military Balance 1989-90*, London: Brassey's, 1989; Arkin, W.M. and R.W. Fieldhouse, *Nuclear Battlefields*, Cambridge, Massachusetts: Ballinger, 1985; press reports.

12 CRACKDOWN

'A custom loathsome to the eye, hateful to the nose, harmful to the brain, dangerous to the lungs' King James I of England, 1601-1625

'A plague, a mischief, a violent purger of goods, and health: hellish, devilish and damned tobacco, the devil and overthrow of body and soul'. Robert Burton, *Anatomy of Melancholy*, 1621

Cocaine, like tobacco, is close to being the ideal consumer product. It is easy to
produce, refine and transport, easy to use and, once used, hard to drop. It is a truly

global commodity which has hardly begun to realize its marketing potential. Like tobacco was at one time it is illegal.

Ninety-eight per cent of the world's coca, the raw material for the drug, is grown in Bolivia, Colombia and Peru. Over the last 30 years, production has risen thirty-fold – from about 16,000 tonnes annually to a maximum of 480,000 tonnes today. About 1.5 million people work directly in the industry – as growers, refiners, distributors and security guards. Many more derive employment indirectly from it by providing goods and services, including covert protection. The industry accounts for nearly half of Bolivia's income from exports, a fifth of Colombia's and an unknown but large proportion of Peru's. There are thought to be about 15 million consumers of cocaine worldwide, spending somewhere between US$30 and 75 billion each year. Two-thirds of them are in the USA.

One approach to the industry was exemplified in September 1989 by Guillermo Larco-Cox, then Peruvian Foreign Minister, when he proposed to the UN General Assembly that cocaine should be legalized, that coca farmers be provided with alternative ways of earning a living, that the transition be funded by buying up the coca crop, and that Peru's foreign debt be transformed into resources for breaking up the drug cartels. He is neither the first nor the last to propose this sort of programme; several governments insist that economic incentives are part of any anti-drug effort. But in practice the world has dressed right with the alternative US approach: criminalize the business – consumers, traders and producers alike – and bond it to crime, violence, public corruption and private misery, while bribing the weakened producer states with military aid to fight a market force which will not go away and which they cannot overcome.

The commercial realities are simple: in 1989 the USA provided $65 million worth of military aid to Colombia's anti-drug war; coincidentally, it forced a drop in the price of coffee which cost Colombia $500 million in export earnings; it also provided most of the $1.5 billion Colombia earned from cocaine exports. When such market conditions shape the economic decisions made by peasants – whether to grow difficult, uncertain coffee or easy, always profitable coca – the outcome is easy to understand, despite the consequences at the end of the distribution chain.

Sources for map and note:

Panos Institute, *Beyond Law Enforcement: Narcotics and Development,* February 1990; Laffin, J., *The World In Conflict 1990: War Annual 4,* London: Brassey's, 1990; Harkavy, R.E., *Bases Abroad: The Global Foreign Military Presence,* Oxford: Oxford University Press, 1989; press reports.

13 PAX PACIFICA

The Pacific – a vast ocean, thousands of islands, bordered by the Asian and American continents; a major region of military deployment and testing; an area of enormous natural marine resources which is being fished out and polluted.

The Pacific Ocean was the region through which US power first expanded in the 19th century, on its way to Japan, China, the Philippines and later to Southeast Asia. Hawaii was a major staging post which became absorbed into the USA. Other islands became important during World War II in the Pacific campaign against Japan, and found a new use as sites for nuclear testing in the late 1940s. As the technologies of communications, surveillance and long-range missiles developed, the Pacific islands became more important in the eyes of US policy-makers, whether or not they were inhabited. Inhabitants were displaced if they lived too near to testing zones and poisoned if they were not far enough away, their lives and livelihoods reshaped to fit US military convenience. The French and British followed suit in a smaller way, and then the USSR and Chinese, but no other military apparatus can compare with the USA's in the Pacific.

The environmental damage caused by nuclear testing and accidents is severe, yet so far it has not exacted its full penalties. Some islands have been made near-permanently uninhabitable. The very structure of Mururoa Atoll has been irredeemably destroyed by French nuclear tests. There have been protests: by the Pacific island people, by Greenpeace, by some governments. They have done what they can; it has not been enough. When the Greenpeace ship, *Rainbow Warrior,* was destroyed by French agents in 1985, killing one person, the act symbolized what has happened to the Pacific and its **103** indigenous people.

The South Pacific Nuclear Free Zone Treaty (the Treaty of Rarotonga) which entered force in 1986 is an effort to assert a basic right. But the Protocols attached to the treaty, available for the nuclear weapon states to sign as a means of signalling their intent to respect the terms and intentions of the treaty, have been signed only by China and the USSR. France and the USA, the states which bring nuclear weapons into that part of the Pacific, have held themselves aloof.

Sources for map and note:
Arkin, W.M. and R. Fieldhouse, *Nuclear Battlefields,* Cambridge, Massachusetts: Ballinger, 1985; Arkin, W.M. and J. Handler, *Naval Accidents 1945-1988,* Neptune Paper no. 3, Washington DC: Greenpeace Institute for Policy Studies, 1989; Hansen, C., *US Nuclear Weapons: The Secret History,* Arlington, Texas: Aerofax, 1988; Harkavy, R.E., *Bases Abroad,* Oxford: Oxford University Press, 1989; Hayes, P., L. Zarsky and W. Bellow, *American Lake,* Harmondsworth: Penguin, 1987; International Institute for Strategic Studies (IISS), *The Military Balance 1989-90,*London: Brassey's, 1989; *Pacific Research,*quarterly journal of the Peace Research Centre, Australian National University, Canberra various issues; Stockholm International Peace Research Institute (SIPRI), *World Armaments & Disarmament: SIPRI Yearbook, 1968-69, 1974, 1975, 1977,* Stockholm: Almqvist & Wicksell, 1970, 1974, 1975, 1977; *SIPRI Yearbook 1985,* London: Taylor & Francis, 1985; *SIPRI Yearbook 1989, 1990,* Oxford: Oxford University Press, 1989, 1990.

14 END OF EMPIRE

The 1979 census in the USSR recorded 92 different national groups. The largest, at over 137 million, was the Russians; the smallest was the Aleuts, living on the Kormandorskiye Islands off the Kamchatka peninsula, who numbered 441. That so many different nationalities live within the borders of the USSR is a product for the most part not of Soviet-style communism, but of the Tsarist empire's expansion from the late 15th century until the early 20th. Territorial acquisitions by Stalin were mostly re-acquisitions of lands which had been under Russian dominion before the 1917 revolution but which had gained independence immediately after it. Of major territory, only Finland was not regained.

Lenin described the Russian empire of the Tsars as a 'prisonhouse of the peoples', which is how it remained, despite the revolutionary rhetoric of national self-determination, when it became the USSR. When Mikhail Gorbachev decided that in order for economic reconstruction (*perestroika*) to work it had to be possible for people to find a way to voice their opinions and make them felt (*glasnost*) long repressed voices of nationalism were among the first to be heard.

Thus what began as a programme to revitalize the economy and was soon extended to become a process of steady democratization, has paved the way for the possible disintegration of the USSR. Each month brings more signs of an impending break-up: declarations of independence in the Baltic republics; proclamations of greater autonomy in Moldavia, Ukraine, Uzbekistan and the Russian Republic; ethnic clashes in Azerbaijan, the Armenian enclave of Nagorno-Karabakh, the central Asian republics; anti-Moscow demonstrations almost everywhere (including Moscow). The economy is slowing. Official Soviet statistics show the USSR's growth falling from about 8 per cent per year in the late 1960s, to about 3.5 per cent in the first half of the 1980s. The US Central Intelligence Agency estimates a decline from 5 to just under 2 per cent. Independent Russian economists paint a darker picture: a fall from 4 per cent in the late 1960s to virtually zero growth by 1985, when Gorbachev came to power. Since then the position has become even bleaker.

Gorbachev is perhaps the most far-sighted and civilized leader the Russian empire has ever had. For that very reason, he may be its last.

Sources for map and note:
Kochan, L. and R. Abraham, *The Making of Modern Russia,* 2nd ed., Harmondsworth: Penguin, 1983; Kozlov, V., *The Peoples of the Soviet Union,* London: Hutchinson, 1988; Symons, L., ed., *The Soviet Union: A Systematic Geography,* London: Hodder & Stoughton, 1983; press reports; Directorate of Intelligence, *Revisiting Soviet Economic Performance under Glasnost: Implications for CIA Estimates,* Washington DC: Central Intelligence Agency, Sov 88-10068, September 1988.

15 THE LESSER POWERS

Like the superpowers, Britain, France and Cuba have bases a long way from home. Far-flung military deployments are the last vestige of the global empires once ruled by France and the UK. In the 1970s, Cuban forces began to be deployed in Africa and the Middle East in support of Soviet policies. Other states which deploy forces abroad do so primarily in neighbouring countries (see Map 16: The Local Powers).

In their imperial heydays, the British global military apparatus was more extensive, but France has retained a larger post-imperial presence. Before sending forces to the Gulf in August and September 1990, the UK had 20,000 military personnel in the Third World and France roughly 36,000. By superpower standards these forces are not large, but they are widely dispersed. In the number of territories in which they have bases, Britain approaches and France exceeds the USSR, though both are far outstripped by it in numbers of people and equipment (see Map 11: The Superpowers).

French and UK foreign-based forces may be relatively modest but they are still significant. The leftovers of empire involved both states in war during the 1980s: France in Chad and, at lower levels of intensity, in its Pacific possessions, and the UK in the Falkland Islands.

It is not only in the remnants of empire that British and French forces are deployed. At the end of the 1980s, each one's largest single foreign contingent was in West Germany where the UK had nearly 69,700 personnel and France 52,500. The end of the Cold War and the unification of Germany which completes the post-1945 settlement, however, will probably reduce those commitments.

Cuba is the third of the lesser powers, but may not be for much longer. Its military presence in Africa is being reduced; its 40,000 troops in Angola will have been completely withdrawn, if all goes to plan, by July 1991 and its forces in Ethiopia are also shrinking.

Definitions of bases and of communications and intelligence installations for this spread are the same as for Map 11: The Superpowers, and are explained in the note to this map. Comments there about the limitations of the data on foreign military presence are equally relevant here. In particular, there appears to be no accessible information about French intelligence installations; it must be assumed that such facilities exist in many of the states and territories which host French forces and communications stations.

As in Map 11, we have excluded intelligence installations based at embassies, and likewise multinational peacekeeping forces (see Map 3: Force for Peace). We have included French bases and installations in all territories outside metropolitan France, whatever their formal status. We have not, however, included British forces based in Northern Ireland.

Sources for map and notes:

Harkavy, R.E., *Bases Abroad: The Global Foreign Military Presence*, Oxford: Oxford University Press, 1989; International Institute for Strategic Studies (IISS), *The Military Balance 1989-90*, London: Brassey's, 1989; press reports.

16 THE LOCAL POWERS

There are superpowers: with military bases, facilities and installations across the world (Map 11). There are lesser powers with forces deployed far from home (Map 15). And there is a group of local powers, whom we deal with in this map, which base some forces outside their territory, usually rather close to their own borders.

There are three major patterns visible in the foreign basing of the local powers. One we have categorized as 'expeditionary', primarily associated with war and its aftermath. Examples are Moroccan forces in Western Sahara; Israeli, Syrian and Iranian forces (Revolutionary Guards) in Lebanon; Iraqi forces in Kuwait. A different and perhaps more benign example is found in Africa where neighbouring states have given aid to Mozambique to help them resist the banditry of the Mozambique National Resistance (MNR) guerrillas. But expeditionary forces are not only associated with war. Fundamentally, they are about power; the ends of power may be achieved by means of war, but sometimes they are achieved simply by showing or even merely implying the willingness **105** to go to war. That can be enough to stake a convincing territorial claim - or at least to join the competition, as in the Spratly Islands (see Map 10: The Valley of the Skulls) – or shape the policies of another state, especially a small neighbour.

The second pattern we categorize as 'alliance', for example, Belgian, Canadian and Dutch forces in West Germany. While these bases may be just as closely connected to war as expeditionary forces are, or at least to its possibility, they are less closely related to questions of power. (The Hague does not have leverage over Bonn because Dutch forces are in northern Germany.)

The third pattern is in some ways a sub-set of the second, for it involves the stationing of forces in order to indicate alliance, but the forces are not combat-ready; they are in training camps or acting as support units. Examples of this pattern are the foreign military presences of West Germany and Singapore.

We have included the small Dutch presence in Curaçao in the first category. Unassuming as it may seem in the 1990s, some centuries back it was part of the generalized European conquest of the world in which the Dutch played no small part. We have also included the West African force sent to Liberia in the middle of 1990 in the expeditionary category even though the governments which established it described it as a peacekeeping force. Because its presence was not requested by all parties to the conflict (see Map 3: Force for Peace), it did not meet the United Nations' criteria of peacekeeping operations. Whatever words may be used to describe it, only by exerting a decisive influence on the outcome of the Liberian bloodbath could it serve any function at all.

We have, however, perhaps surprisingly, defined the forces sent to Saudi Arabia after the Iraqi invasion of Kuwait as alliance rather than expeditionary forces. This reflects the symbolic and subordinate role these forces were playing in August and September 1990. As events develop, so may the meaning of a foreign base, in these or any other circumstances.

Sources for map and notes:

Harkavy, R.E., *Bases Abroad: The Global Foreign Military Presence,* Oxford: Oxford University Press, 1989; International Institute for Strategic Studies (IISS), *The Military Balance 1989-90,* London: Brassey's, 1989; press reports.

17 BEFORE THE THAW

The international order which was initiated after World War II and is now ending was heavily though never exclusively bi-polar. By the mid-1950s, through its major alliances – the North Atlantic Treaty Organization (NATO), the Central Treaty Organization (CENTO) and the Southeast Asian Treaty Organization (SEATO) – together with a number of bi- and tri-lateral alliances, the USA had established and dominated a worldwide network of military and political coalitions. Its basis was both military and economic might (see Map 11: The Superpowers). The USSR – weaker economically and with a more restricted military reach – worked on a similar pattern with the Warsaw Pact and, later, bilateral friendship and cooperation treaties through which it gained bases and/or provided military aid, equipment and advice.

Many states consistently expressed the intention of remaining outside the bi-polar system. By the end of the1980s, 100 states formally claimed non-aligned status. But the reality is that not many managed to be genuinely non-aligned, partly because of the ties formed between their armed forces and those of either the USA or, in fewer cases, the USSR. Those that did achieve effective non-alignment include the two most populous states – China and India. Other states which managed it include those in Europe which built on a long tradition of neutrality, such as Switzerland and Sweden, or opted early on for non-involvement in the East-West conflict, such as Finland, Ireland and Yugoslavia. In other cases, non-alignment has been a product of establishing ties with both East and West (a pattern adopted by some Third World states – Peru, Malta and others) or rigidly with neither (Albania). In the case of Austria, non-alignment is a result of the agreements under which the occupying powers withdrew their forces ten years after the end of World War II.

The bi-polar order was never absolutely stable. Several states changed sides – Cuba,

Egypt, Indonesia among them – as a result of changes in the nature of the state or merely in state policy. Others switched from alignment to non-alignment, the most notable example being China's break from the USSR.

The end of the Cold War was initiated by a series of changes in Soviet policy. These began in arms control and continued in 1989 even more dramatically, with the USSR's acceptance of change in central and eastern Europe. Less noticed, except in the case of its withdrawal of combat forces from Afghanistan, the USSR also turned away from its previous policy of attempting to multiply its friendship treaties with Third World states, a policy which many Soviet strategists believe had given it little except an added economic burden. Consequently by mid-1990, the Soviet system of alliances was in total disarray. The Warsaw Pact, cornerstone of the system, was steadily disintegrating and military support to what had formerly been key Third World allies had diminished.

This process has not been matched on the US side. Though CENTO fell into disuse and SEATO disbanded, and despite challenges to US alliance leadership from, for example, France in the 1960s and New Zealand in the 1980s, and though its dominance in NATO over key policies weakened at the very end of the 1980s, the overall shape of the US system is intact.

In the long-term change seems inevitable. US leadership of NATO has been largely dependent on the western European states' perception that they needed the USA to defend them against the USSR. As the Soviet threat evaporates, so may US influence in Europe erode. That process may be hastened and extended both by economic rivalry from the USA's major allies in western Europe and Japan, and by the costs of sustaining a worldwide military apparatus in the face of huge federal budget deficits, a national debt climbing well beyond the three trillion dollar mark (on which the interest payment is above three per cent of annual economic output), and large trade deficits.

But even if change is on its way it will probably be slow and uneven. In the Gulf crisis after the Iraqi invasion of Kuwait, the first signs were seen of a new configuration of military alliance and deployment. Out of that may come a renewed basis for the USA's allies accepting its strategic leadership.

The map focuses on military ties which, in the case of links with the USA or its major allies are usually accompanied by a similar economic orientation. These factors say far more about a state's real alignment (or lack of it) than rhetorical claims to non-alignment, votes in the UN or attendance at the non-aligned movement's conferences.

The nature of the ties varies from case to case. Some are major security alliances. Most others on the US side are agreements to host forces, or allow them access, or on the supply of equipment, or provision of training and advice; on the Soviet side, they are in general treaties of friendship and cooperation, under which the provision of bases, training and equipment is agreed. We have judged whether a state is a major ally of either superpower on the basis of its membership of one of the major alliances, or because of its particular weight in the USA's or USSR's strategy and policy. Some states have agreements and ties with the USA which are less important than those they have with Britain or France, and we have accorded them a different status on the map.

States we have described as effectively non-aligned are ones which have military ties with neither side of the bi-polar system, or equally with both, or whose agreements are less important than other elements of long-standing strategic policy. Unavoidably we have had to exercise judgement in deciding, for example, whether Iraq's agreements with the USSR qualify it as a Soviet ally, or whether (as we concluded) its long-standing policies merited its inclusion among the effectively non-aligned. The states shown as members of the non-aligned movement are those which attended the 1988 Nicosia non-aligned conference, plus seven who usually attend but did not in 1988. Namibia is shown as a member by virtue of the attendance at Nicosia of the South West African People's Organization. The Palestine Liberation Organization is also a member.

Sources for map and note:
International Institute for Strategic Studies (IISS), *The Military Balance 1986-87*, London: International Institute for Strategic Studies, 1986; *Treaties in Force - January 1 1988*, US Government Printing Office, 1989; Morphet, S., 'The Non-Aligned Movement and the Foreign Ministers' Meeting in Nicosia', *International Relations*, Vol. IX, No. 5, May 1989; press reports.

18 UNCOMMON EUROPEAN HOME

An American journalist reports on Poland after the end of Communist rule and finds it less than a bed of roses: '"You don't get it, do you?" Piotr Bikont, the documentary-film maker, said to me one evening after I had spent half an hour voicing my forebodings - ecology, union busting, exploitation. "Yes, of course, those are all real problems," he said. "Real problems. But that's the point – they're the real, normal problems of real, normal countries. You have no idea how long we've been yearning for real, normal problems instead of all the surreal abnormal problems we've had to cope with in this crazy country for so many years."'

That view of Poland can be extended to the other Warsaw Pact countries and perhaps to Europe as a whole. After more than 40 years of being the focal point of Cold War, of being the site of the world's largest but, by the end, largely ritualized military confrontation, the upheavals of 1989 should let 'real, normal problems' emerge to dominate the political agenda.

The items on it have been placed there in part by four decades of unreal, abnormal problems. Large parts of the continent are an ecological disaster area, especially in central and eastern Europe. Dismantling the arsenals will take time, effort and the imagination to develop new concepts of security which are not based on confrontation with either old or new enemies. The extent of NATO's ability to accommodate the new reality of life without its traditional enemy was unclear in 1990. France and the UK were both continuing to modernize and expand their nuclear arsenals and, though military reductions and withdrawals appeared to be the general order of the day, there were plans in NATO to bring in a new generation of air-launched nuclear missiles.

But the agenda is also shaped, perhaps decisively, by a different set of issues which raise question marks about the future of the traditional state in Europe. States are caught between the scissor-blades. On the one hand, economic integration reaches a milestone in 1992 with the introduction of the single market in the countries of the European Community (EC). On the other hand, pressure is building up from national and ethnic minorities for greater rights, regional autonomy and, in some cases, secession.

The demands of the supra-national economy have not only strengthened and expanded the economic role of the EC, they also make it a magnet for other European economies, and will likely extend its political role as well. Four national economies dominate the EC which dominates Europe. Whether that will lead to political domination - and if so, whether by the EC as a whole, by a consortium of the four, or by one state alone - is a question which may get an answer in the 1990s.

Not all the actors are states. Within the shift to a larger economic and political unit - the EC - there is also multiple pressure to shift to smaller units, to develop greater regional autonomy. Europe is a patchwork of nationalities and ethnic minorities. Only part of it is shown on the map where we focus on the political representation of nationalism and demands for ethnic rights. We have not displayed - because they do not put the same pressure on the state – those groups which, though ethnically recognizable, are not so politically organized. Among them one can count the Vlachs of northern Greece, the Sorbs of southeastern East Germany, the Saami of northern Finland, Norway and Sweden, the 5 million Roma people of 22 countries and many other groups. Nor does the map show immigrant minorities such as the Turks in Germany, or the Arabs in France, or the Asians, Africans and Afro-Caribbeans in the UK, or the Indonesians in the Netherlands, or others. Nor does it show the Jewish communities or those areas where demands for autonomy are based on regional rather than national or ethnic identity.

This patchwork creates a much richer and more varied Europe than is seen if we look only at state borders. It reveals the artificiality of the term 'nation state', of its borders and even of the very idea of it. The determination with which minorities cling to their identity and assert their rights can be explosive and murderous; some areas are already dangerous and others may become so. But that determination could also be fruitful in a Europe which must find new ways to ensure that 'real, normal problems', do not lead to 'real, normal' injustices and conflicts.

Sources for map and note:
Minority Rights Group, *World Directory of Minorities*, Harlow: Longman, (1989-90); *Economist* 'Survey of the European Community', 7 July 1990; Arkin, W.M. and R.W. Fieldhouse, *Nuclear Battlefields*, Cambridge, Massachusetts: Ballinger, 1985; Harkavy, W.M., *Bases Abroad*, Oxford: Oxford University

Press, 1989; International Institute for Strategic Studies (IISS), *The Military Balance 1989-90*, London: Brassey's 1989; Wechsler, L., 'A Reporter at Large: A Grand Experiment', *New Yorker*, 13 November 1989; press reports.

19 KILLING POWER

When the casualty figures of current wars are contemplated (Map 29: The Butchers' Bill), it is salutary to reflect that the weapons which caused them constitute a tiny proportion of the world's destructive potential.

There are many ways to compare overall military strength; some of the outline information needed for these comparisons is available in this atlas. The most common way is by numbers: of equipment (see Maps 21: Conventional Power and 23: Nuclear Fix), or of military personnel (Map 33: Under Arms), or of money spent on the military (Map 36: What Peace Dividend?). The types of equipment available must also be included in the comparison (see Maps 21 to 24). The nature of the military apparatus may also be gauged by taking into account how it is deployed (Maps 11: The Superpowers, 15: The Lesser Powers and 16: The Local Powers). In this map we compare total destructive power and, equally innovatively, in the next we compare war space.

None of these measures, however, can permit conclusions to be drawn about relative military effectiveness in combat except of the very grossest kind. They have more to say about the use of human and physical resources in military preparations - and the lengths to which different states have gone - than about military effectiveness.

The method and information on which this map is based are both inevitably arbitrary. The technique was developed by an historical research unit in the US Department of Defense in the 1960s and 1970s as an instrument for war-gaming - for simulating combat in order both to predict outcomes and design forces more efficiently. It represents one of the few systematic attempts to quantify the lethality of weapons and forces in a way which is comparable across time and between different types of weapons - hand-to-hand combat and multi-megaton thermonuclear bombs both have their places on the lethality index.

'Lethality' is best understood as 'deliverable destructiveness'. It encompasses not only, for example, the explosive power of a shell, but also the distance over which it can be fired, with what degree of accuracy, at what rate of fire and how reliably. It includes armoured protection (if any) and (if it is a mobile system such as a tank or aircraft) mobility and endurance. Each of these elements in the calculation is given a 'weighting'; that is, it is given a numerical value which reflects its assumed importance. This weighting appears largely to be derived from empirical study of the actual effect of weapons in battle. For the purposes of comparison, the period of time in which the weaponry is used is one hour, and the lethal effects are calculated on people standing in the open.

A lethality calculation is made for each weapon and weapon system, and the total for all armaments in the forces of any state can then be calculated. This is what we have done.

Before these figures could be used to predict the outcome of conflict, a series of variables would have to be introduced to account for the effects of such factors as weather, terrain and the different demands of defensive and offensive operations. Detailed information would also be required on the deployment of the opposing forces - how many would be available on which battle fronts, for example - and their tactics. Even then, it is not clear that this method can adequately account for other important elements which decide the outcome of battles: the strategic and tactical acuity of the leaders; the morale and skill of the led; the proportion of equipment which has been properly maintained and will perform to expected levels, compared to the proportion which has been shoddily maintained; the difference between how equipment performs in test and battlefield conditions.

The system puts a strong emphasis on pure firepower at the expense of, for example, very fine accuracy. This bias, together with the necessary working assumption that equipment will perform as well as expected, may partly explain why the map shows the USSR with nearly one-and-a-half times as much lethality as the USA. It is also worth **109** noting that the system appears to have been developed primarily for battles on land; it is not clear how far it can be applied to naval armaments, aerial warfare, long-range nuclear missiles and bombers or chemical warfare.

These methodological issues pale, however, alongside the problems of data. Detailed information on the capabilities and performance of weaponry is far from comprehensive, nor is there full information on every aspect of every state's armed forces. Where holes existed in the data, we filled them by inference from comparable weaponry, or from armed forces structured in the same way as those of a state on which the facts were incomplete. At some points, inference descended into guesswork, though it was often informed and always modest.

Several decisions about how we treated the data are relevant. In general, only frontline combat forces and their currently operational equipment were included; that is, reserve forces and stored and reserve equipment were excluded. As exceptions to this rule, we included the Revolutionary Guards of Iran, the Citizen Force of South Africa, and the mobilized army strength (i.e. including reserves) of Austria, Israel, Sweden, Switzerland and Yugoslavia. No allowance was made for the degree of readiness of forces and their equipment, except in the case of submarine-launched ballistic nuclear missiles.

As well as the five declared nuclear weapon states (USA, USSR, UK, France, China), Israel and South Africa were credited with having nuclear weapons but not India or Pakistan (see Map 23: The Nuclear Fix). In the case of the European NATO states which would have access to nuclear weapons in war, that firepower was added to their lethality totals, not to the USA's, though it is the latter state which has custody of the warheads and shells in peacetime. For weapon systems capable of delivering either nuclear or conventional weapons, we counted as nuclear only that number for which, on available information, nuclear explosives are available. We excluded from the totals US and Soviet nuclear weapons being withdrawn under treaty agreement, but in all other cases the data used derive from mid-1989 and therefore do not reflect reductions in armed forces which have been undertaken since.

With chemical warfare weapons (CW), almost all the data (except for the physical effects of gas weapons) had to be inferred or estimated. Estimates of the USSR's stockpile of toxic gases, for example, have ranged from 30,000 to as high as 800,000 tonnes; we worked from the USSR's official statement that it has 50,000 tonnes of gas stored in bulk and weapon-form, and estimated how much of each gas was ready in what type of munitions, using information released at the Geneva Conference on Disarmament. For the USA, the range of estimates is narrower - 30,000 to 32,000 short tons in bulk and weapon-form; we estimated the distribution of its arsenal on the basis of information also released at the Conference on Disarmament. For Iraq, CIA estimates of its capacity to produce CW weapons were scaled down by reference to historical experience of the proportion of production capacity which is actually utilized. This gave us an estimate of how much gas Iraq has. We estimated the distribution of the arsenal on the basis of data gleaned from UN studies of Iraqi use of CW weapons against Iran. In all three cases, the calculating basis of the methodology - the amount of destruction which can be delivered in one hour - meant that the lethality calculation considerably understated the total destructive potential of the CW arsenals.

In the end, we shrugged at all such limitations of data and methodology. The result is, inevitably, impressionistic. Even so, it reveals the extent of the 40-year-long obsession of the USA and, even more, of the USSR with piling up destructive machinery. Many other states have been and are now obsessive in seeking destructive potential; none, thankfully, has matched the superpowers.

Sources for map and note:
Dupuy ,T.N., *Numbers, Predictions & War,* London: Macdonald & Jane's, 1979; Dupuy, T.N., 'Weapons Lethality and the Nuclear Threshold', *Armed Forces Journal,* October 1978; Kaldor, M. and J.P. Perry Robinson, 'War' in *World Futures,* Freeman, C. and M. Jahoda, eds., International Institute of Strategic Studies (IISS), London: Martin Robertson, 1978; International Institute of Strategic Studies, *The Military Balance 1989-90,* London: Brassey's, 1989; Glasstone, S. and P.J. Dolan, eds., *The Effects of Nuclear Weapons,* 3rd ed., Tunbridge Wells: Castle House, 1980; Goodwin, P., *Nuclear War: The Facts on Our Survival,* London: Ash & Grant, 1981; Arkin, W.M., T.B. Cochran and R.S. Norris, *The Bomb Book,* New York: Natural Resources Defence Council, 1987; Spector, L.S., *The Undeclared Bomb,* Cambridge, Massachusetts: Ballinger,1988; Robinson, J. P. Perry, 'World CW Armament', *Chemical Weapons Convention Bulletin,* Autumn 1988, May 1989; Robinson, J.P. Perry,

'The Chemical Industry and Chemical Warfare Disarmament: Categorizing Chemicals for the Purposes of the Projected Chemical Weapons Convention', The Chemical Industry and the Projected Chemical Weapons Convention, Stockholm International Peace Research Institute (SIPRI), *Chemical & Biological Warfare Studies* no. 4, Oxford: Oxford University Press, 1986; Carus, W.S., *The Genie Unleashed: Iraq's Chemical and Biological Weapons Production,* Washington DC: Washington Institute for Near East Policy, 1989; Reports of the United Nations Investigatory Teams in Iraq and Iran, 1984, 1986 and 1987 in Dunn, P., *Chemical Aspects of the Gulf War 1984-1987,* Australian Department of Defence, Materials Research Laboratories, 1987, Conference on Disarmament Documents CD/789, December 1987, CD/830, April 1988.

20 THE KILLING FIELDS

Most life inhabits a very narrow zone reaching 100 metres into the air, 2 metres into the land, 10 metres below the surface of the oceans and 2 metres above the ocean bed - a total of 55.6 million cubic kilometres. Some forms of life are encountered further afield: up to the limits of the troposphere (say, 11 kilometres on average) down to the bottom of the oceans (an average of 3.2 kilometres) and, at most, 2 kilometres into the earth's surface. Taking the most generous limits, and ignoring the dead bits in between, this gives us a biosphere of 7,063.2 million cubic kilometres.

The outer reaches of the human war zone – the space in which the military can routinely operate - stretch very much further at present: from the operating height of a military satellite (say, 35,000 kilometres) to the operating depth of a nuclear-powered submarine (say, 0.3 kilometres) and a bomb-crater depth of 0.2 kilometres. The total is 19,360,138 million cubic kilometres – over 2,600 times the volume of the biosphere as broadly defined.

And this is without accounting for the effects of poisoning with radiation and chemicals, or the collateral effects of firestorms producing enough smoke to cause artificial eclipses of the sun (the nuclear winter). In short, it is a calculation of war space which is necessarily incapable of encompassing the element of time.

Only the USA and the USSR command the full human war space. A few other states - the UK, India, France, Spain, Italy and Brazil (some way behind) and Argentina (just about included in this group) - fall short of that but still claim war space larger than the world's living space. China's warspace is, surprisingly, not part of this group, limited perhaps because it has neither strategic missiles nor aircraft carriers.

Measuring war space is not without complications. We have taken the significant dimensions for normally effective military reach to be:

Length
40,000 kilometres for nuclear-powered submarines, aircraft carriers, battleships and cruisers, arbitrarily halved to allow for the land masses (under 30 per cent of the world's surface);
20,000 kilometres for conventional submarines, with the same proviso;
10,000 kilometres for inter-continental and submarine-launched ballistic missiles (ICBM and SLBM);
3,000 kilometres for medium-range ballistic missiles, destroyers and frigates;
2,000 kilometres for bombers (adding 1,000 kilometres for in-flight refuelling capacity).

Height
35,000 kilometres for military satellites;
14 kilometres for fighter planes;
3 kilometres for surface-to-air missiles (other than strategic);
1 kilometre for air-defence guns.

Depth
300 metres for nuclear-powered submarines and for anti-submarine armaments;
200 metres for conventional submarines.

We have also assumed, sometimes in defiance of evidence to the contrary (in Cambodia, Ethiopia, Lebanon for example) that all states can wage war over the whole of their claimed territory up to a minimum height of 200 metres, and can mount a thrust of 300 kilometres beyond their own borders (one refuelling, of seven hours at 40 kph, in **111** average conditions on land, and most of the 370 kilometres - 200 nautical miles - claimed as their Exclusive Economic Zone by most maritime states).

None of this implies that states have undisputed sway over their war space. On the contrary, war spaces are in principle shared: totally, in the superpowers' case, partially in all other cases. Even diminutive Nauru with its 60 cubic kilometres of war space contends with the colossi, the superpowers with more than 17 trillion (17,000,000,000,000) cubic kilometres, as well as with some of the other major players.

War spaces have expanded astonishingly in the past 40 years and, even more remarkably, the cost of claiming a stake has widely, although not uniformly, plummeted. The superpower space warriors have multiplied their war spaces more than 27,000 times and reduced its annual cost per cubic kilometre by more than 99.99 per cent. The more earth- and sea-bound major players have expanded war spaces by an average of 87.5 per cent, reducing unit costs by 99.5 per cent. For the remaining states, whose combined war spaces have increased by only 50 per cent at most, and which have been squeezed by ever-rising weapons prices, the costs of claiming war space have risen steeply, by 75 per cent. Entry into the nuclear and space ages is expensive, often prohibitively so.

As measured for 1949, war space is fairly notional. There were no missiles and no nuclear-powered naval craft. We assumed a range of 1,000 kilometres for all bombers and a ceiling of one kilometre for air combat and air-defence. We ignored submarine warfare. In order to have a basis for comparison, we organized the data as if all the states which existed in 1988 did so in 1949.

Sources for map and note:
International Institute for Strategic Studies (IISS), *The Military Balance 1989-90,* London: Brassey's, 1989; 'World Missiles', supplement to *Defense and Foreign Affairs,* Alexandria, Virginia: March 1989; Lovelock, J.E., *Gaia: a New Look at Life on Earth,* Oxford: Oxford University Press, 1979; *McGraw-Hill Encyclopaedia of Science and Technology,* New York, 1982; Taube, M., *Evolution of Matter and Energy on a Cosmic and Planetary Scale,*Springer Verlag, 1985.

21 CONVENTIONAL POWER

The major weapons depicted in this map represent only a fraction of conventional military power. Unlike the weapons of mass destruction (see Map 23: Nuclear Fix and Map 24: Bugs and Poisons) they are the weapons of current war, the instruments of current deaths. But they are, of course, stockpiled not only for war but also for defence, challenge and the self-glorification of states or state leaders.

When the Cold War ended, the USSR owned the world's largest conventional stockpile with more than three times as many tanks as the USA, and 70 per cent more major warships. In combat aircraft, the figures are much closer. The data for this map come from 1989, at which time neither disarmament negotiations nor unilateral reductions had made much of a dent in the Soviet arsenal. Though the USSR was then, and, until it manages to get rid of several thousand items of military hardware, will remain, the world's major conventional power, several other states have built large arsenals.

It is worth repeating a point made in the note to Map 19: Killing Power: numbers alone do not adequately measure comparative military strength. For such an exercise it would also be necessary to take into account factors such as the quality of equipment, the degree of training and experience of the people who would use it, the tactics of its use and the morale of conflicting forces. The purpose of this map is to identify which states direct most resources to producing or buying conventional weapons, thus making those resources unavailable for other uses - whether for industrial growth or for attempting to deal with such scourges as famine, malnutrition, pestilence, illiteracy and environmental degradation.

'Combat aircraft' are primarily intended to deliver munitions against targets in the air, on land or at sea; the term excludes training, reconnaissance, transport and tanker aircraft. An 'aircraft carrier' is a ship which carries fixed-wing combat aircraft (that is, not just helicopters and small spotter aircraft). The number each carrier can take varies from case to case; the range is from less than 10 to as many as 90. 'Major warships' are

state. India is believed to have the essentials for assembling 50-60 warheads at short notice, while Pakistan is thought to be able to do so on a much smaller scale. All four of these states can be regarded as *de facto* nuclear powers even though only one of them is known for certain to have crossed the threshold and assembled nuclear weapons.

The actions of several other states reveal that they have, at the least, kept their nuclear weapon options open during the 1980s. None of them is currently thought able or likely to exercise the option very quickly, and some of them, especially those in the Middle East, are probably several years away from being able to manufacture nuclear weapons. But such judgements are tenuous. It appears now that Israel had nuclear weapons several years before the rest of the world began to suspect. When the first hard information was leaked from inside Israel's nuclear bomb factory by Mordechai Vanunu, it emerged that the Israeli arsenal was both bigger and technically more sophisticated than had been previously thought.

Even if they are never used in war, nuclear weapons pose enormous risks. Though atmospheric nuclear testing has been stopped, underground nuclear tests can and do 'vent' radiation into the atmosphere, for example, the British test in Nevada, USA. Accidents also occur while nuclear weapons are in transit: over 15,000 are deployed at sea, others are transported by air or on land to and from bases. There have been 212 reported accidents involving nuclear-powered vessels since the first was launched in 1954. The US Navy has reported that it experienced 630 accidents involving nuclear weapons between 1965 and 1985. Known accidents at sea include sinkings, vessels running aground, collisions, submarines snagging trawlers' nets and surfacing under civilian or military vessels, mechanical breakdown, leaks of primary coolant, radiation leaks, explosions and implosions. There have also been several hundred accidents on land and in the air. Many were what the US military classifies as 'incidents' - near-misses, crashes, fires and other occurrences which are viewed as having created no dangers for people or the environment – but some caused deaths and/or radioactive pollution.

In very few cases has information about these accidents been willingly provided by official sources. In numerous cases, the truth has been distorted and downright lies are far from unknown. In all cases, nuclear states predictably try to play down the risks involved in any accident involving their own forces. The gruesome calm of official utterances may be most tellingly illustrated by the British Ministry of Defence, commenting on an incident in which a fitter at the Chatham dockyard inhaled radioactive material: 'He feels no ill effects and seems to be well'.

The map shows only the most serious of known military nuclear accidents. It must be assumed that it is an incomplete record.

Precise figures on nuclear warheads can only be estimated; their real numbers are not known. US and Soviet figures have been rounded to the nearest 1,000. For Britain, France and China, they have been rounded to the nearest 25. The range of estimates for Israel's nuclear arsenal stretches from 50-60 to 100-200; we chose 100 as a convenient compromise. For South Africa the range of estimates is from 20 to 40, depending on several unknowns – whether it has actually assembled warheads and, if it has, with what design; given this uncertainty, 25 seemed a moderate and even modest estimate. Britain now has its own nuclear warheads as shown on the map, but in the event of war, would also have access to US warheads. In October 1990 the Brazilian government disclosed the full extent of previous nuclear weapons research and promised to end it.

Sources for map and note:
Arkin, W.M. and R.W. Fieldhouse, *Nuclear Battlefields,* Cambridge, Massachusetts: Ballinger,1985; Arkin, W.M. and J. Handler, *Naval Accidents 1945-1988,* Neptune Papers no. 3, Washington DC: Greenpeace Institute for Policy Studies, 1989; Cochran, T.B. et al, *The Bomb Book,*Washington, DC: Natural Resources Defense Council, 1987; *Defense Monitor,*1981, no. 5, Washington DC: Center for Defense Information; Hansen, Chuck, *US Nuclear Weapons: The Secret History,*Arlington, Texas: Aerofax, 1988; International Institute for Strategic Studies (IISS), *The Military Balance 1989-90,* London: Brassey's 1989; Spector, L.S., *The Undeclared Bomb,* Cambridge, Massachusetts: Ballinger, 1988; Stockholm International Peace Research Institute *World Armaments and Disarmament: SIPRI Yearbook,*eds.:1968-69, Stockholm: Alqvist & Wiksell 1970; *SIPRI Yearbook1974, 1975,1977* Stockholm: Almqvist & Wickell, 1974; 1975, 1977; *SIPRI Yearbook 1985,*London: Taylor & Francis, 1985; *SIPRI Yearbook1989,* Oxford: Oxford University Press, 1989.

aircraft carriers, battleships, cruisers, destroyers, frigates and submarines; the term excludes corvettes, mine-laying and mine-detection vessels, coastal craft, amphibious warfare vessels and landing craft. 'Main battle tanks' are heavy, tracked tanks; all other armoured fighting vehicles, of which there are many thousands, are excluded.

Sources for map and note:
International Institute for Strategic Studies (IISS), *The Military Balance 1989-90*,London: Brassey's, 1989.

22 22 THE GREAT EQUALIZER

From February to April 1988, Iran and Iraq launched between them, 500 to a thousand ballistic missiles at each other's cities. The resulting carnage created a new focus of concern for those who worry about the international arms trade.

In the 1970s anxiety was focussed on supersonic combat aircraft; today it is on surface-to-surface ballistic missiles with ranges above 40 kilometres. These weapons - especially the longer-range ones – threaten to be the great 'equalizers' in global killing power. States which have them, whether supported by the West (Iraq, 1980-89) or not (Iraq, 1990), could make the sort of long-range strikes of which once only the superpowers and a few of their allies were capable.

But there has been no great proliferation. These types of missile were owned by 30 states in 1980, 32 states by 1989. But that relative stability masks two trends. First, Third World states are acquiring missiles with longer ranges, able to hit targets hundreds rather than tens of kilometres away. Second, more states are acquiring the technological capacity to develop missiles, either by themselves or together with other partners. Map 28: Psst! provides more information on the ways in which - and the partners with which - missile development is spreading.

Most of the missiles in the 1989 inventories were rather inaccurate in their targeting. That too is likely to change. And several states outside NATO and the Warsaw Pact now have the ability to add chemical or nuclear warheads to their missiles, dramatically increasing their killing power (see Map 23: Nuclear Fix and Map 24: Bugs and Poisons).

The arsenals depicted on this map exclude surface-to-surface missiles deployed for coastal defence or on ships for use in war at sea. Five states own coastal defence missiles, while shipborne missiles are owned by 68 states. No distinction is made on the map between nuclear, chemical and conventional warheads. Though Iran owns missiles made in the USSR, it is possible that it purchased them from North Korea. That is only one example of the blurred edges of the available data on missile forces.

Sources for map and note:
Carus, W.S., Evidence before the House Foreign Affairs Committee, US Congress, 12 July 1989; Carus, W.S., 'Missiles in the Middle East: A New Threat to Stability', *Policy Focus,* Research Memorandum no. 6, Washington DC: Washington Institute for Near East Policy, June 1988; Shuey, R. D. et al , *Missile Proliferation: Survey of Emerging Missile Forces*, Washington DC: US Congressional Research Service, 3 October 1988; International Institute for Strategic Studies (IISS), *The Military Balance 1989-90*, London: Brassey's 1989.

23 NUCLEAR FIX

The end of the Cold War virtually eliminated the risk of thermonuclear war between the superpowers, but that does not mean an end to the problem of nuclear weapons. The US-Soviet treaty on Intermediate Nuclear Forces - signed in December 1987 and ratified the following year - was the first superpower agreement to reduce nuclear stockpiles, but the weapons it covered carried less than 2,000 warheads out of a world total of well over 50,000. Moreover, not all 2,000 warheads will be eliminated. Some will be 'recycled' for use on other missiles. Further negotiations on strategic nuclear weapons - the Strategic Arms Reductions Talks (START) under way in 1990 - could eliminate perhaps another 9,000 warheads.

Only five states acknowledge that they own nuclear weapons. But incontestable evidence shows that Israel has nuclear warheads for its Jericho missiles, and the
114 balance of evidence points very strongly to South Africa too being a nuclear weapon

24 BUGS AND POISONS

Virtually all weapons are chemical in one sense or another, and all chemicals are toxic in certain quantities. There are, however, weapons whose lethal effect depends on their toxicity: these are what most people call chemical weapons and what we have pedantically chosen to call 'weapons for chemical warfare' or 'CW weapons'.

As with long-range missiles (Map 22: The Great Equalizer) so with CW weapons; it was the war between Iran and Iraq which emphasized a new threat of proliferation. Having used poison gas against Iranian forces, Iraq also used them against Kurdish civilians.

These are two of only three authenticated uses of CW weapons since the end of World War II. But accusations that CW weapons have been used, or are possessed, or are being developed, have become quite frequent, entering the ordinary discourse between hostile states.

The technology of CW weapons is well within the reach of numerous Third World states as well as all industrially advanced ones. Manufacture is hard to identify and prevent because lethal weapons can be made from the same constituents as insecticides, and in the same sort of factories.

This is partly why there is so much uncertainty about which states have or are developing CW weapons. Most of the allegations of ownership or development recorded on the map stem initially from US intelligence. But US intelligence officials are inconsistent and contradictory in their statements about how many (and which) states have chemical weapons capacity, whether they are known or suspected to have it, and whether the capacity amounts to possession of a militarily usable weapon or to the potential for making such a weapon in the not too distant future. The range of estimates by US officials from 1988 to 1990 goes from six states having CW weapons, to as many as 25 which are known or suspected to have or be developing them.

Some statements made with apparent certainty are later implicitly contradicted without being explicitly retracted. Libya, for example, was the target of numerous accusations throughout the 1980s – that it had CW weapons, that it had used them, was about to use them, was making them. In late 1988, the US government announced that Libya had constructed a plant at Rabta to make CW weapons and in early 1990 announced it had started producing them. It would seem that the Rabta accusations rendered all the previous ones null, but at no time did the US government acknowledge error in its earlier claims.

Technical identification difficulties apart, there are also problems of ideology and the demands of state policy. Libya was the target not only of a US bombing raid in 1986 but, throughout the 1980s, of an especially intense diplomatic campaign.

The most dramatic example of uncertainty about CW weapons ownership, however, is France. For years it was widely believed to possess gas weapons, if only because of the studied ambiguity of its statements. In 1988 President Mitterrand denied that France owned chemical weapons. In the absence of firm evidence to the contrary -evidence which is conspicuously lacking in relation to these weapons - France is now widely believed not to possess CW weapons.

Most allegations that CW weapons have been used are made either by survivors of an attack (or by people alleged to have survived the alleged attack) or by forces fighting against the accused state, or by authorities which, though not directly involved, are *parti pris*.

In the 1980s the most notorious case was the 'Yellow Rain' affair, in which the Vietnamese forces in Laos and Cambodia were alleged to have used poison gas. Analysis of samples of foliage brought out of Southeast Asia, the US State Department claimed, supported the case. Further independent analysis indicated that the CW weapon in question was, in fact, bee excrement. There was no scientific basis to the allegation, and it seemed the testimony of 'victims' was unreliable either because of genuine confusion, or because they were simply lying at somebody's instruction. We do not include it on the map. The allegation against Vietnam which we do show is a different case. The evidence is made up of accounts by deserters. How reliable they are, we are not qualified to judge. That there is some supporting evidence does not amount to proof.

Of those cases classed as allegations backed by evidence but not proven, the one most nearly proven is the Iraqi claim that Iran had used gas. A UN investigation team found Iraqi soldiers who had clearly been victims of gas, but their report left room for doubt as to whether it was Iranian. They could have been accidental victims of their own army's gas attacks, their suffering then exploited in an effort to support the claim that Iran had used gas as well as Iraq. That Iraq used gas was not only proven by the UN team but later acknowledged by the Iraqi regime.

These doubts about the Iraqi claim, or doubts about other claims, do not mean we are dismissing them. Nor does the inclusion of an allegation in the map mean that we endorse it. Though we have excluded a small number of accusations which would seem to be simply antagonistic diplomatic froth, we have tended to included most allegations and have not attempted to judge their authenticity. It is by no means impossible that allegations for which there is evidence are false, and allegations for which there is no evidence are true.

In 1990 a draft Chemical Warfare Convention was being prepared at the Conference on Disarmament in Geneva. It reflects an international effort to ban CW weapons which has been gathering momentum since the mid-1980s. It remains to be seen whether it will lead to CW disarmament by the USA, USSR and Iraq and prevent CW proliferation.

Bacteriological weapons (or biological or germ weapons) possibly arouse even deeper fears than gas weapons. For a long time, the Biological Warfare Convention was the only agreement for actual disarmament between the USA and the USSR; it was first signed in 1972 and entered into force in 1975; it was not until the Intermediate Nuclear Forces Treaty, signed in 1987 and ratified the following year, that the superpowers made another agreement to get rid of some of their weapons. Despite frequent US accusations that the USSR was continuing to research bacteriological weapons during the 1980s, and despite infrequent accusations made against a handful of other states, it does not appear that these weapons are in any states' arsenals at present. That may be due to the inherent difficulties of controlling them if used.

Sources for map and note:
Sussex/Harvard Information Bank on CW weapons; Stockholm International Peace Research Institute (SIPRI),*World Armaments & Disarmament: SIPRI Yearbook*, successive eds. 1980-89; *Chemical Weapons Convention Bulletin,*Issue 5, August 1989; SIPRI data; press reports.

25 THE ARMOURERS

It takes more than manufacturing to make weapons. As with any complex technological product, the process begins with the initial concept, proceeds through the design, research and development to production and testing of prototypes, and finally to full production. Each stage in the process requires a particular technological and industrial capability - scientists and technologists with the appropriate skills, the necessary equipment, materials and factories.

No state takes every weapon it uses the whole way through that process. Even the superpowers, albeit sparingly, import, copy and customize equipment. The more a state depends on its own capabilities, the less dependent it is on other states for equipping its armed forces. On a spectrum of dependency, there are several significant, though often elusive, distinctions. Importing everything means total dependency on outside suppliers. Carrying out final assembly of foreign design with foreign industrial help barely qualifies the degree of dependency, but assembling the finished product without outside help marks a step towards independent industrial capabilities. A further step is marked by the capability for research and development (R&D), which can modify designs made in another state (see Map 35: Mind Out). More independent still is an R&D capability which generates its own designs, less independently if working with foreign boffins, more independently if working without them.

In the leading armourer states, the place at which any project is located on that spectrum is almost entirely a matter for choice. The mix between differently located projects can also be chosen. For states with less military industrial capability, freedom of choice is more constrained. For those with no such capability, there is no such freedom; if such states want weapons they must buy them, or invest in the capability with which to develop them. This latter can be and has been done. South Korea, in the third category on our map, is clearly a candidate for the second, while Japan could easily upgrade to the first. The barriers between the different stages are by no means impenetrable, though passing through is expensive and diverts industrial and technological abilities and resources away from civilian production.

Our mosaic of the armourers' world is made up from the number of weapons manufactured (main types only, excluding variants) in 42 categories towards the end of the 1980s. The categories are:

Main battle tanks & medium tanks; light tanks; tank destroyers & anti-tank vehicles; armoured cars, reconnaissance vehicles & scout cars; armoured personnel carriers & infantry fighting vehicles; self-propelled & towed artillery; self-propelled & towed anti-aircraft systems; multiple rocket systems; unguided anti-tank weapons; machine guns; mortars.

Nuclear-powered ballistic missile submarines; nuclear-powered cruise missile submarines; ballistic missile submarines; cruise missile submarines; nuclear-powered attack (hunter-killer) submarines; attack (hunter-killer) submarines; aircraft carriers; battleships & battle cruisers; guided-missile cruisers; guided-missile destroyers; destroyers; guided-missile frigates; frigates; corvettes; fast attack craft; amphibious warfare vessels; mine warfare vessels; naval guns; surface skimmers; torpedoes.

Aircraft; flying training aircraft.

Strategic missiles; cruise missiles; surface-to-surface missiles; air-to-surface missiles; anti-ship missiles; anti-submarine missiles; surface-to-air missiles; air-to-air missiles; anti-tank missiles

The organization of categories is, of course, open to qualification and challenge. Any attempt to classify something as blurred of definition as industrial capability must be indicative at best. By focussing on the breadth of equipment categories, however, we believe we have achieved a valid classification of the world's armourers.

As more and more states produce weapons and equipment, so more and more sell them on the world market. In consequence, the number of states hosting arms exhibitions swells, to the discomfiture of the established exhibitor state, the despair of the exhibitor companies and the dismay of the professionals. 'We can easily imagine the dilemma facing the manager of a medium sized industrial company,' wrote the editor of the *International Defense Review* (IDR) in December 1986. 'Is there a way out?' he asked. As it happened, there proved to be none. Two and a half years later, the IDR commented, 'By their sheer number, defense exhibitions have turned from a welcome marketing event to an often onerous commitment.'

Our data for the inset 'War Fair' come from the IDR. We have tinkered with its data to a limited degree by including states where there are regular exhibitions even if they are not annual.

Sources for map and note:

Chant, C., *A Compendium of Armaments and Military Hardware*, London/New York: Routledge & Kegan Paul, 1987; *International Defense Review*; press reports.

26 THE ARMS SELLERS

If domestic arms production allows a state some freedom of action (see note to Map 25: The Armourers), exports are often necessary to make it possible. They increase the volume of production of a particular item of hardware, thus reducing overall unit costs, and keep the industry occupied when domestic demand has been met. In effect, they recruit the world to share the producer's fixed overheads. For this reason alone the inducement to export is nearly irresistible.

Although most of the major exporters attempt not to sell to potential enemies, they consistently get it wrong: British sales to Argentina before the 1982 war over the Falkland Islands; French sales to Iraq in the 1980s; US sales to the Shah of Iran in the 1970s (the equipment was still there when he was overthrown by a religious movement **117** which believed the USA was the world's Great Satan). Despite all this experience, states continue to sell weapons abroad, hoping that today's customer is tomorrow's friend (and repeat customer), but unable to guarantee it.

We can only guess at the size of the international arms market. More than ten years ago, the Stockholm International Peace Research Institute (SIPRI) wrote, 'There is no exact, reliable or even reasonable information as to the real value of the international arms trade.' Despite SIPRI's own heroic efforts, little light has since been shed on the matter, although a small one flickered in eastern Europe in 1989-90 when the extent of covert sales by East Germany and Czechoslovakia emerged briefly into the open as their Communist regimes were swept aside.

We have taken SIPRI's figures as the best available. They are the product of independent, disinterested research (unlike the tendentious statistics of the US Arms Control and Disarmament Agency), the only practicable alternative source. SIPRI's data are couched in dollars of constant value, which allows for comparison across time. Though more extensive than most other available data, SIPRI's cover only major, big-ticket items. The widely traded smaller weapons do not feature, nor, of course, the clandestine 'black' and 'grey' international arms markets (see Map 28: Psst!). There are also gaps in SIPRI's data on military spending, especially for China and the USSR. This point is significant for the graphic on the ratio of exports to domestic production because our estimates include a rule of thumb judgement that approximately 40 per cent of military budgets is spent on weapons procurement. We treated lacunae in military spending data in the same way as for Map 36: What Peace Dividend? For an explanation, see the note to that map.

Sources for map and note:
Stockholm International Peace Research Institute (SIPRI), *World Armaments & Disarmament: SIPRI Yearbook 1990,* Oxford: Oxford University Press, 1990.

27 THE ARMS BUYERS

Through the 1970s and into the 1980s, world arms exports grew alarmingly fast. It was alarming for those who worried about peace. It was also alarming for those who worried about the diversion of wealth away from dealing with problems of hunger, poor health and lack of a basic social infrastructure in Third World countries. In the latter part of the 1980s, exports began to shrink, not because the world was becoming more peaceful, but for three other reasons.

The first was that even the most spendthrift were running out of money. The legacy of their earlier spending spree, and of the hard-sell of the exporters, was overstocked arsenals and a heavy burden of debt. Repayments on the latter do not come from those whose liking for the advanced technology of war and power led their governments into debt. Instead, economic austerity programmes squeeze resources from the poorer sectors of society, from those who are least able to pay and who have played no part in the decision to buy arms on credit in the first place. Weapons can kill without being used. The second reason that arms exports began to shrink is that even when states were not strapped for cash many of them had almost no room for new purchases. There are limits to what armed forces can absorb; particularly rich Third World states often exceed them, but even the crassest reach saturation level sooner or later. The third reason is that several states, of which the outstanding example is Iraq, used imports as part of a programme of steadily building up their own military industrial capability (see Map 25: The Armourers and associated note).

The cartogram shows the main importers, who make up some 80 per cent of world demand. Comments on the availability of reliable data made in the note to Map 26: The Arms Sellers apply equally here.

Sources for map and note:
Stockholm International Peace Research Institute (SIPRI), *World Armaments & Disarmament: SIPRI Yearbook 1990,* Oxford: Oxford University Press, 1990.

28 Psst!

It is not surprising that there is little public information about the international black and grey markets in weapons. Some of its participants are famous: Sam Cummings, a native of the USA and citizen of the UK who operates from both those countries; Adnan Khashoggi, a Saudi Arabian who was involved in the Lockheed bribes scandals of the 1970s and the clandestine US sales to Iran in the 1980s which produced the Irangate affair; Albert Hakim, an Iranian-born US citizen who also figured in the Irangate deals; Sarkis Soghnalian, an Armenian operating from Miami. But all their business dealings are intended to be confidential. It is a trade that operates in a shadowy world of numbered Swiss bank accounts, back-handers and front companies.

The overall size of the market is completely unknown and no guess-timate is worth making. The annual turnovers of the companies headed by the best known individuals reportedly run into several tens of millions of US dollars. According to *Fortune* magazine, Ernst Werner Glatt, a West German, got rich by selling weapons bought from Warsaw Pact states to the mujahadeen in Afghanistan and to the contras in Nicaragua; his business is estimated to have a US$200 million annual turnover. The hallmark of the trade is disrespect for ideologies and the deepest respect for the laws of the market.

Also instructive is the career of Gerald Bull, Canadian born, naturalized American, who was murdered in Brussels in March 1990. Shortly after his death he appeared on the front pages of the world's press. Components of the 'supergun' he had designed were discovered on their way from British factories to Iraq. Bull had once been a contractor for the US Department of Defense; after the Pentagon decided it did not want his 'supergun', he sold extended-range artillery to Israel and to South Africa in the 1970s.

A typology of the trade would include several different kinds of deal. There is, firstly, straightforward trading in hardware, though usually not the major weapon systems which adorn the arsenals of the superpowers. There are large markets for both new and second-hand items. Supply lines often take circuitous routes to evade inconvenient export restrictions and to mask the deal from prying eyes. There is also a flourishing market in equipment syphoned off from military arsenals. In the mid-1980s a group of US Navy employees simply walked off with aircraft and missile spare parts from the depots. The goods, worth several million dollars, were sold to Iran.

Secondly there is a large trade in the equipment and machinery needed to develop, produce and test weaponry. This is often exported quite openly, with the end-use designated as civilian. The multiple applications of, for example, very sophisticated computers often make this designation quite credible, even to the exporters. Corporations involved in the clandestine arms trade are not always aware of it. Supplies from many sources are stitched together to provide, for example, Iraq or Libya with the capacity to make chemical warfare weapons. Knowledge of the overall shape of the process and its purpose is tightly restricted.

There is also the practice of trading through front companies. This was adopted, for example by Italian and German companies in order to cover up their supplying of missile technology to states in the Middle East. The use of front companies was also adopted by the Iraqi government to enable it to purchase arms-related industrial equipment in Europe.

Such deals come to light in a variety of ways: through investigative journalism; through occasional lapses in security by suppliers, intermediaries or purchasers; and through the increasingly close watch kept by western intelligence on trade in some technologies (especially missiles and CW weapons) to some states - especially in the Middle East. But the trade remains largely clandestine, supplying the arsenals of fighting forces, equipping anybody from tyrant to guerrilla, turning a fast, large and secret buck. In the recorded views of most of its known participants, it is no different from the more public trade in armaments recorded in Map 25: The Arms Sellers and Map 26: The Arms Buyers, except that it is done more quietly. This map records deals which have surfaced in the public domain, that is, a very small part of the trade.

Sources for map and note:
Adams, J., *The Unnatural Alliance,* London: Quartet, 1984; Carus, W.S., *Evidence before the House* **119**

Foreign Affairs Committee, US Congress, Washington DC, 12 July 1989; *Chemical Weapons Convention Bulletin,*various issues; Dowd, A.R., 'How U.S. Arms Dealers are Making a Killing', *Fortune,*16 February 1987; Jaster, R.S., *The Defence of White Power,* London: Macmillan/International Institute for Strategic Studies (IISS), 1988; Spector, L.S., *Going Nuclear,*Cambridge, Massachusetts: Ballinger,1987; Sussex/Harvard Information Bank on CW Weapons; press reports.

29 THE BUTCHERS' BILL

It is impossible to have more than the vaguest idea of the number of dead and wounded in current wars. Estimates are often plucked from the air by desk-bound journalists far from the scene of fighting; equally often they are plucked from the 'information' agencies of one or other combatant and then packed with propaganda purpose by protagonists and commentators. They can vary alarmingly or, what is equally disconcerting, remain rigidly fixed. Were a million people slaughtered in Cambodia under the Khmer Rouge in 1975-1978? Or was it two million? Clearly rounded to the nearest million, both figures have been used and both given credence. At the other end of the scale, the available figure for Israeli deaths in war from 1948 to 1988 is 16,500: this figure covers Jews only - how many Arabs are uncounted is anybody's guess.

The nature of war has changed. There was a time when most wars were formal, structured and distinct, and when most casualties were combatants. Their fate and whereabouts were the responsibility of the military organizations. In World War I, for example, some 95 per cent of the 10 million fatalities and 20 million wounded were directly engaged in fighting. Now wars are much more diffuse. By and large they do not start and end on definable dates (see the note to Map 4: The Dogs of War). In this modern style of war, about 90 per cent of casualties are thought to be non-combatant civilians beyond the immediate purview of a responsible authority (should there be one). They are difficult to identify and do not enter into reliable statistics of death and violence.

In some cases, the impact of war shows through in population statistics which vary significantly from previous estimates of population growth. The method is shaky, of course: population growth estimates are notoriously inaccurate, not least in war-ravaged states, and projections are undermined by spontaneous changes in fertility and indirectly attributable mortality, as well as by direct war deaths and forced emigration. It is also difficult to choose a base year for projections, not least because wars do not necessarily have a clean and clearly identifiable starting date. Nonetheless, where actual population change has varied widely from earlier projections, we may conclude that some desperate upheaval has occurred. And often we find the name of that upheaval is war.

Sources for map and note:

Brogan, P., *World Conflicts,* London: Bloomsbury, 1989; Sivard, R.L., *World Military and Social Expenditures 1989,* Washington DC: World Priorities Inc, 1989; Wallensteen, P., ed., *States in Armed Conflict 1988,* Department of Peace and Conflict Research, Uppsala University, Report no. 30, Uppsala, Sweden, July 1989; Population Reference Bureau Inc,*1989 World Population Data Sheet,* Washington DC; *World Demographic Estimates and Projections 1950-2025,*New York: United Nations, 1988.

30 THE DISPLACED

'Contemporary history has created a new kind of human being - the kind that are put in concentration camps by their foes and internment camps by their friends.' Hannah Arendt

At the beginning of the 20th century, civilians constituted five per cent of war casualties; at the end they constitute around 90 per cent. One consequence of civilian populations becoming targets in war is panic and flight.

In ordinary parlance, a refugee is somebody who has left home involuntarily for fear of persecution, injury or death and who would go back if it were possible or safe to do
120 so. There are hundreds of million of such refugees, newly huddled in the world's cities,

swarming across frontiers and oceans, attempting to escape from violence and destitution, famine and discrimination.

But the official language in which refugees are discussed and defined is no ordinary language. The subjects it normally recognizes are relatively few: people who have fled their country (not just their home) and who receive official aid. It does not recognize those who have been forcibly relocated - to 'homelands' in South Africa, or from the Kurdish areas in Iraq, or from possible war zones in Ethiopia or from their ancestral villages in Ceausescu's Romania. It does not recognize 'returnees' - Jews to Israel, 'ethnic Germans', or the übersiedler going from East to West Germany. It does not recognize those who have been dispossessed - by colonizers in Brazil or Indonesia, or by planners in most Third World states. It does not recognize 'economic migrants' - the Vietnamese 'boat people', Mexican 'wetbacks', the 50,000 Africans slipping illegally in to Italy every year, the 800,000 North Africans in Spain. It does not recognize the hundreds of thousands of ordinary people leaving Iraq and Kuwait in August and September 1990. It does not recognize the million or so shanty-town dwellers around Buenos Aires and the similar numbers in many Third World cities.

And beyond these restrictions, the official language establishes a hierarchy in which people 'in need of protection and/or assistance' are more deserving than people 'in refugee-like circumstances'. 'Internal refugees' are a privileged sub-category of 'the internally displaced'. Both are distinguished from the most privileged - the cross-border refugees. Welcome or not, miserable or happy, the refugee who has 'entered and resettled' in a new country is dropped from the register.

The statistics that survive these semantic wars are articles of faith and flags of convenience. Host states typically exaggerate the number of the 'externals' they harbour in order to extract the maximum foreign aid; aid agencies do the opposite to protect their budgets. Everyone tries to deny the existence of 'internals'.

The production of refugee figures in Somalia is typical. The flow of refugees into the country followed its defeat at the hands of Ethiopia in 1978. By 1981 the Somali government claimed there were 1,300,000 in camps and 700,000 elsewhere. The UN High Commission for Refugees countered with a range of between 450,000 and 620,000. A compromise 'planning figure' of 700,000 was agreed in 1982 which was raised to 840,000 after a new influx in 1984-85. Referring to the first half of the 1980s and created by an unreal negotiation, these figures naturally diverge from those shown in Map 7: The Thorn of Africa. The statistical war in Somalia was marked by the equivalent of forced marches as truck-loads of non-refugees were transported from camp to camp. To prevent refugees from registering more than once, they were stained with chlorine. Donors failed to provide all the food they had pledged and what was received was distributed selectively by the government.

Refugees are created. It is the state that creates them, primarily through war, but also through the incidental effects of war, through discrimination short of systematic violence, or through sheer bad husbandry. And it is the state that we hold to account. For this reason we have reversed the conventional presentation which focuses on states as refugee asylums: we prefer to show states as refugee generators.

Not that states wish to compete as asylums. As the refugees multiply they find it increasingly difficult to go forth legally, not to say with any semblance of dignity. Switzerland, which accepted about 70 per cent of applicants for refugee status in the 1970s, ended the 1980s with a seven per cent acceptance rate. France took 60 per cent in 1983, but 30 per cent in 1987. The UK dropped from 41 per cent in 1982 to eight per cent in 1987. According to the UN High Commissioner for Refugees, acceptance rates were down to 7-14 per cent overall by the end of the 1980s. And more and more traditional asylum states were adopting temporary expedients short of acceptance: it is called 'tolerance' in West Germany, 'exceptional leave to remain' in the UK.

No wonder there have come into being whole refugee societies in the Middle East, Cambodia (and across the border into Thailand), Hong Kong, Zambia and elsewhere: people born in refugee camps of people themselves born in refugee camps and who, occasionally, as in Lebanon, have been compelled to flee those camps - refugees a second time round.

Sources for map and note:
World Refugee Survey, US Committee for Refugees, annual; Washington DC; press reports.

31 MILITARY RULE

Armed forces are everywhere the ultimate guarantor of a state's authority within its borders. Where the apparatus of government and authority is incapable of maintaining the political and social order, the military are often tempted to step in, not to guarantee but to usurp the state's authority. Where it has happened once, it may happen again; some armed forces enjoy the habit of power and develop a tradition and an expectancy of intervening in politics. In several Latin American countries, in parts of Africa, in Pakistan and the Philippines and elsewhere in Asia, the military have assumed special political rights.

There are various military roles in government. In military regimes, the forces govern openly through a military chain of command - as in Sudan, for example. Such states are the exception. There are more military-dominated states where power is in effect exercised by the military, although this reality is obscured by the existence of a civil constitution, a seemingly independent judiciary, or even competing political parties and elections. In such states the military dispose of the important departments of state - typically defence and internal security - or occupy the presidency or its equivalent, or do both. Among the many and different states in this group are Algeria and Somalia, El Salvador and Paraguay, Thailand and Indonesia.

The overwhelming majority of states are not military in either of these pronounced ways. In most states the military influences the exercise of state power but does not control it. In some - Israel or Argentina, for example - that influence extends to the power of informal veto over state policy; in others - Austria or Japan, for example - it is scarcely noticeable. Such military influence always exists. We do not remark upon it on the map.

Sources for map and note:
Keesing's Record of World Events, Harlow: Longman; ABECOR Country Reports; Central Intelligence Agency (CIA) Directorate of Intelligence, *Chiefs of State and Cabinet Members of Foreign Governments,*Washington DC: CIA September/October 1989; *International Who's Who,* London: Europa Publications, annual.

32 OFFICIAL TERROR

As stated in the note to Map 5: Unofficial Terror, if terrorism consists of targeting a victim or engaging in violence in order to influence the behaviour of others, often unnamed or unknown, all states are terrorists. Even if the term is confined to extra-legal acts, states still emerge as the greatest terrorists of all.

At the end of the 1980s no fewer than 51 states - about 30 per cent of the total - were reported as currently resorting to extra-judicial killing or abduction ('disappearances'). These are the *assassin* states. Many of them, in some macabre trade-off, had foresworn judicial killing (capital punishment). Some had abandoned it altogether - such as Colombia, Ecuador, El Salvador, Haiti, Honduras, Nicaragua, Panama, the Philippines and Venezuela. Some eschewed it in all but exceptional circumstances - such as war, in the cases of Brazil, Israel, Mexico, Peru and Sri Lanka. It had simply been stopped in practice by others - such as Guatemala, Lesotho, Madagascar, Morocco, Nepal and Suriname.

The *assassin* states are joined by another 64 *torture* states. In the United Nations definition, torture 'means any act by which severe pain or suffering, whether physical or mental, is intentionally inflicted by or at the instigation of a public official on a person for such purposes as obtaining from him or a third person information or confession, punishing him for an act he has committed, or intimidating him or other persons. Torture constitutes an aggravated and deliberate form of cruel, inhuman or degrading treatment
or punishment.'

*Declaration Against Torture,*adopted unanimously by the United Nations, 9 December 1975.

In a further 10 *lawless* states, arbitrary arrest, trial, detention or exile were sufficiently commonplace to constitute a normal instrument of state policy. The three categories together total 125 states, 72 per cent of the world's total.

Some states are clearly more frightful than others. Iran or Iraq, for example, where state-instigated killing, torture and general lawlessness are lavishly used to uphold the interests and dignity of the ruling group in every particular, are part of a different league from Australia, West Germany or others where such activities are officially condemned, sometimes condoned or quietly encouraged and only exceptionally prescribed. Nor is there much point in ignoring the real differences between states such as the UK and USSR, in which official mayhem is rationed, and the likes of India where it is freely available. However, state terrorism is so corrupting of society and human values that it should not claim a place in the world under any circumstances. In any case, differences in scale within a hierarchy of frightfulness blend into each other so subtly and secretly that an attempt to order them would create distinctions where none exist. Accordingly, the map distinguishes between different types of state terrorism, but does not add further quantifying distinctions.

We have singled out capital punishment explicitly used for political purposes - as retribution for crimes against the state - from capital punishment carried out for attacks on individuals or private property. The states which carry out most executions - China, Iran, Iraq, Nigeria, Somalia and South Africa - use capital punishment as much for political reasons as for maintaining public order.

Nothing coarsens the official conscience so much as the imposition of its views by force. So states that have had recent experience of civil war are likely to be the ones where people have the least rights. We have identified them on the map.

In nearly all cases, the *assassin* states are also the *torture* states and they, in turn, are also the *lawless* states. Occasionally our sources report on the worst abuses and not on the lesser ones. In such cases - Australia, the Bahamas, Gabon, Grenada, Hong Kong, the Maldives - we have taken the reported instance to cover all lesser denials of human rights. Australia, for example, is included in the second category as a *torture* state because of its brutal treatment of aboriginals in custody, although no other breaches are noted in our sources.

The map contains surprises. It is simply incredible, for example, that Mongolia - a hardline Stalinist regime during the period covered - should be among the handful of states with a clean record on human rights. The explanation is that the record is empty rather than clean. Information simply did not come to the notice of our sources.

Sources for map and note:
Amnesty International (AI) Report 1988,1989, London: Amnesty International, annual; *When the State Kills: The Death Penalty v. Human Rights,* London: Amnesty International, 1989; US State Department, *Country Reports on Human Rights Practices for 1988,*Washington DC: US House of Representatives, 1989; *Critique: Review of the Department of State's Country Reports on Human Rights Practices for 1987,* New York: Human Rights Watch and Lawyers' Committee for Human Rights, June 1988.

33 UNDER ARMS

The relative size of armed forces, and the proportion of each country's young male population that serves in them, reveal more about the nature of each state than about the effectiveness of its forces. Military service diverts people out of productive activity. Worldwide, armed forces serve as much to bolster the prestige and internal authority of the state as to provide national security from external threat, but even when large forces can be justified by a state's strategic situation, the global consequence of employing over 35 million people in this way is enormous wasted potential.

The vast majority of military personnel are young men. In looking for a way to assess the 'population density' of armed forces country by country we rejected comparisons with overall population figures which include a majority of people who are too old or too **123** young to serve. Of the age bands available for comparison, the 18-32 bracket for men seemed the most appropriate. It includes the age at which men are liable to conscription in countries where that applies, as well as the ages of a considerable number of military personnel who serve longer terms. It is a flawed and rough measure but useful for comparing states' consumption of young energies.

Using an age band of men does not mean we ignore the part played by women, who have long been employed in an auxiliary role in some states' forces. In recent years they have also moved into combat roles. While there is a logic in this - equal rights and equal responsibilities extending into the military - one has to wonder whether an equal right to kill is a right worth striving for; whether it is, in fact, a right in any worthwhile sense at all. Little information is available about women in the armed forces. As well as the 12 countries shown on the colour strip, our source reports women in the regular armed forces of four other states - China, Israel, Mozambique and the USSR - without giving numbers.

The term 'para-military' is elastic. It covers a wide variety of organizations - riot police, other special police units, border guards, internal security troops, coastguards - and is not used consistently by all countries. We have excluded local militias and other part-time units. Thus the information on the cartogram sometimes understates the full extent of the military and para-military presence.

The source for this map was published in 1989, before reductions in military personnel announced by the USSR and by other Warsaw Pact states had taken effect. As these cuts and further ones negotiated during 1989 and 1990 filter through, they will change the relative sizes of some of the largest armed forces. Important though that is, however, its effect on the global picture should not be overestimated. If all the cuts in the pipeline in early 1990 are implemented, the total of over 35 million people in military and para-military forces will be reduced by only a million or so - less than three per cent.

Sources for map and note:
International Institute for Strategic Studies (IISS), *The Military Balance 1989-90,* London: Brassey's, 1989.

34 OBJECTION

Systematic conscription for military service in the modern era began in 18th century Prussia and, after being adopted by revolutionary France, spread throughout continental Europe. It was adopted by the new states of Latin America and, in the current century, by some former colonies.

Policy and practice often diverge where large numbers are involved. So it is with military service. In some states it is compulsory by law but not enforced - Burkina Faso, Haiti, Honduras, Ivory Coast, Jordan, Myanmar (Burma), Zaire. In others - Nepal, Pakistan - there is a kind of economic conscription: it is voluntary by law, but not readily avoidable for some groups in some districts. In yet others - Mexico, Morocco - voluntary service is backed by selective conscription to make up the numbers. There are some conscription states that formally provide for non-combatant service in the armed forces, and others that do so informally. In all cases where they diverge, we have favoured practice over policy.

States which recognize conscientious objection vary widely in the extent of their recognition. In Bolivia, only Menonites are permitted to be COs; in West Germany, the status of CO is available virtually on demand. States also differ in the way they deal with the objectors they recognize. Britain grants absolute exemption from any kind of service to the few that emerge after they have volunteered for service but reconsidered. In its day, East Germany confined objectors to non-combatant duties in the armed forces. Most states permit alternative civilian service for those whom they recognize as conscientious objectors; many enforce a longer period for civilian service than exists for military conscription, sometimes twice as long.

Objectors are usually obliged to make a formal application to a tribunal before call-up. Only West Germany, the Netherlands and Sweden allow conscripts to claim CO status at
any time before or after the start of their military service. In some states, such as

France, the procedure is so complex and exhausting that it acts as a substantial deterrent. And often tribunals disallow the sincerest of applicants, even though it is obvious that no court can claim superior knowledge of an individual's conscience.

The more repressive a regime, the more likely it is to have conscription without the right to conscientious objection. Iran, Iraq or China, for example, sometimes execute those who refuse military service. Others like South Africa imprison objectors for long periods. There are some states, such as the USSR, which do not recognize conscientious objection officially, but while most objectors are imprisoned a very few religious objectors are sometimes informally permitted to perform alternative service.

In 1987 the UN Commission on Human Rights called on member states to recognize conscientious objection as a human right. Hungary was one of the first states to legislate to that effect, even before the changes which swept through eastern Europe in 1989-90. It is likely that reforms in military service will follow the political changes in the region. In the USSR, the abolition of conscription is under discussion.

Sources for map and note:
Eide, A. and C. Mubanga-Chipoya, *Conscientious Objection to Military Service*, New York: United Nations,1985; International Institute for Strategic Studies (IISS), *The Military Balance 1989-90*, London: Brassey's,1989.

35 MIND OUT

The proportion of military spending on research and development (R&D) may not at first seem hugely significant. It accounted for under three quarters of a per cent of economic output in the USA, the most prodigal state in the first half of the 1980s, its most prodigal years. It amounted to no more than ten per cent of all military spending worldwide. Yet its effects are profound.

Because today's R&D leads to the production of weapons far into the future - a decade or more - it loosens the bonds between weapons acquisition and inter-state relations. Politics and strategic situations may change, but military R&D goes on, the arms industry goes on, the arms race goes on. Thus arms-making is invested with an autonomy that cannot but feed back into political life, affecting attitudes, policies and budgets. In this sense military R & D, unlike its civilian counterpart, helps to create the very problems it purports to solve, and results in expenditure vastly in excess of the amount it absorbs directly.

The USA and the USSR account for about 80 per cent of military R&D; four more states (the UK, France, China and West Germany) are responsible for a further 15 per cent or so. These six states are also the major arms exporters (see Map 26: The Arms Sellers). The effects of their R&D reverberate through the many military systems which buy their advanced weapons.

This cartogram in particular must be seen as indicative rather than definitive. As Mary Acland-Hood, a major authority on the subject, writes: 'The factual basis for analysis of the scale, pattern, implications and effects of military R & D ... is poor: among the problems are concealment, understatement, incompatible or inadequate definitions, uncertainty about the inclusion of much space and nuclear military R & D as well as the general problems that arise with any comparison between countries.'

The estimates on which the cartogram is based were made in the mid-1980s and relate to the first half of the decade. They take no account of subsequent developments such as the emergence of small but increasingly significant bit-players like Iraq and the consequent relative, though still marginal, decline of the superpowers.

We could not have presented our conclusion visually without doing some violence to our sources, by ignoring their qualifications and reservations and by collapsing ranges of estimates into single quantities, the mid-point.

Sources for map and note:
Acland-Hood, M., personal communications; Acland-Hood, M., chapters in Stockholm International Peace Research Institute's *World Armaments & Disarmament: SIPRI Yearbook1983, 1984, 1985*, London: Taylor & Francis, 1983, 1984, 1985; *SIPRI Yearbook1986,1987*, Oxford: Oxford University Press, 1986, 1987; Acland-Hood, M., *Military Research and Development, Resource Use and Arms* **125**

Control,Oxford: Oxford University Press, forthcoming; Jacobson, C., ed., *Estimating Soviet Defence Expenditures,* Oxford: Oxford University Press,1987; Thee, M., ed., *Arms and Disarmament: SIPRI Findings,* Oxford: Oxford University Press,1986.

36 WHAT PEACE DIVIDEND?

Even if we were to get them right, budgetary dollars and cents could never measure the true cost of the military. We could come up with figures on losses due to military action - Ruth Leger Sivard suggests a figure for property losses of US$500 billion due to the seeding of Afghanistan with hundreds of thousands of mines, the bombing of medical centres in Mozambique and Nicaragua, and the defoliation of vast areas of Vietnam. But not even the most nerveless accountant can measure the losses occasioned by traumatizing whole populations, or the cost of disfiguring imaginations and intentions across the world, as a consequence of military spending.

Nor is the measurement of military budgets an easy proposition. They are never fully disclosed, nor in principle can they be, since concealment is part of the very strategy and tactics they are meant to further. And they are wildly resistant to comparison: the freedom of trade in military goods and services, including labour, which is necessary to form a universal measure of value is inconceivable because both the domestic and export markets are so highly politicized. Some sources, including our own, use as their universal measure US dollars of constant value, a measure which is fairly insensitive to the uneven pace of price changes worldwide, thus compounding the difficulties of comparison.

So our figures are at best estimates; though we believe them to be educated estimates. Most of them derive directly or indirectly from the Stockholm International Peace Research Institute (SIPRI), notable for its dispassionate and scholarly detective work on the subject. But SIPRI is a mite too careful for our purposes and its most recent *Yearbooks* omit estimates for some of the biggest spenders, the USSR and China among others. The most serious problem is the relative size of the Soviet military budget. There are two difficulties: knowing its value in roubles and converting this into US dollars for the sake of comparison. Under Mikhail Gorbachev's *glasnost,*some progress has been made on the first. But under the same Gorbachev's *perestroika,* conversion to an international measure - the second problem - has got worse if only because patchy implementation of price reform distorted relative prices more, and more unevenly, than ever before. In fact, the Soviet government, although strapped for every last cent in foreign currency, is reported to be planning a US$25,000 prize for the best rouble-dollar conversion scheme. The prize, however tempting, is unlikely to solve a multi-billion rouble conundrum without the help of full currency convertibility backed by full free trade in goods and services.

For this cartogram we have taken the average ratio of Soviet to US military spending given by SIPRI for 1981-85, before SIPRI gave up providing an estimate for the USSR. Applying that ratio to current US military spending, we produced an initial figure for Soviet military spending. We then reduced this figure by 14.2 per cent, to reflect the unilateral cut in military spending announced by Gorbachev in January 1989. We see no reason to doubt the intentions of a regime under irresistible pressure to pare unproductive spending, or of a political leader who has shown that he does deliver when and where he can. Although the result is a crude estimate so are, in the end, the military spending figures of many more states.

China's military spending is, if anything, even more elusive. The first, interrupted phase of that country's equivalent of *perestroika* has led to even greater confusion. We have adopted and brought forward the lower limit of SIPRI's first guarded estimate of 40-43 billion yuan (US$10.8-11.6 billion) for 1988.

SIPRI has also ceased to provide figures for Vietnam, Cambodia and Laos; we carried forward the imputed average annual share of the area in SIPRI's Far Eastern regional totals for 1981-85. Since SIPRI has not estimated Afghanistan's military spending since 1980, to obtain a figure we carried forward the ratio between Afghanistan's military spending and Sri Lanka's for 1976-80, when figures for both were given, through to 1989 when both were embroiled in widespread civil war in which there had been large scale foreign intervention.

If figures for military spending are shaky, those for the military's share of resources - whether of total economic output or of government spending - are positively flakey. They are affected by intractable conceptual and technical difficulties embedded in the larger sums, as well as by the particular problems involved in estimating military spending.

For the military share of economic output, we have used SIPRI's estimates where possible. In some cases - notably the USSR, the Warsaw Pact and the world total - we used our own estimates of military spending procedures as already described above and applied them to World Bank data and gross national figures as relayed by the *Encyclopaedia Britannica*.

We must confess to having used a most dubious source for the military share of central government expenditure - the US Arms Control and Disarmament Agency. Readers should bear in mind that ACDA compares independently and generously estimated military spending with government budgets that exclude large portions of such spending. In consequence, it greatly exaggerates the burden on the central finances of Warsaw Pact and other (current or former) 'enemy' states. But for all their faults, the figures it produces are at least comprehensive and uniform.

Sources for map and note:
Government Financial Statistics Yearbook 1988, Washington DC: International Monetary Fund, 1989; Stockholm International Peace Research Institute (SIPRI), *World Armaments & Disarmament: SIPRI Yearbook,*successive years, 1986 to 1990, Oxford: Oxford University Press, annual; US Arms Control and Disarmament Agency, *World Military Expenditure and Arms Transfers 1988,* Washington DC: US Government Printing Office, 1989; World Bank, World Tables 1987, Washington DC: World Bank & International Finance Corporation, 1988; World Bank, *World Development Report 1989* ,Oxford: Oxford University Press, 1990; Encyclopaedia Britannica, *World Digest,* annual.

37 AT THE TURN OF THE DECADE

History accelerated at the turn of the decade and made the world more than usually contradictory and confusing. One month, nothing but the end of the Cold War seemed of any importance; the following month, it seemed only the depredation of a depraved dictator had any relevance. There was more peace in some places, but appalling and worsening violence in others. In several countries there was more formal democracy but that did not always mean much more real freedom.

It may be that South Africa encapsulated the contradictions most clearly - as the African National Congress and the apartheid government declared peace with each other, so the Inkatha-ANC war produced a grisly carnage. Or perhaps the Middle East was the place to look to epitomize the changing world, as states which had recently lost one enemy sent their flotillas to the Gulf to confront another. Or perhaps it was the USA where the contradictions came out most strikingly. In 1990 it could no more afford its huge arms budget and massive Federal deficit than it could in 1989. But, with the Gulf crisis, it had a chance to assert itself in a new way by sending tens of thousands of soldiers to the Saudi desert. Somebody, somewhere stopped counting the cost.

At any rate, the turn of the decade was one of those rare moments which defines the next political era. The map does not present a judgement about the nature of the new era. It is a snapshot, a single frame in the middle reel of an epic story. It deals with the major political changes that are related to the end of the Cold War, and with those which are not. It shows which conflicts diminished and which intensified (conflicts which, in our view, remained at the same level of violence are not included).

On this map, we include as 'conflicts' violent confrontations between state and people whch had not escalated to war by September 1990. Their concentration in Africa may suggest where to look for the next historical acceleration.

More than most of its companions, this map is a personal signature. It relies heavily on our personal judgement of what was happening at the time. Its sources are those we have used elsewhere in the atlas, supplemented by anxious searches through each day's newspapers until we were well past our original deadline.